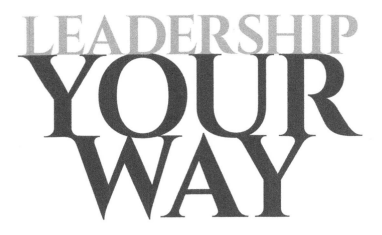

LEADERSHIP YOUR WAY

PLAY THE HAND YOU'RE DEALT AND WIN

KIM KRISCO

ixia
PRESS

Mineola, New York

Bibliographical Note

This Ixia Press edition, first published in 2018, is an updated and revised republication of the work originally published by Miles River Press, Alexandria, Virginia, in 1995.

International Standard Book Number

ISBN-13: 978-0-486-82445-1
ISBN-10: 0-486-82445-4

IXIA PRESS
An imprint of Dover Publications, Inc.

Manufactured in the United States by LSC Communications
82445401   2018
www.doverpublications.com/ixiapress

Dedication

To **you**, and all those who care enough to develop their leadership skills. It's one great way to love the people within your enterprise. And, to the day when you and others might use the word "love" in a business meeting . . . and it will not be unusual or surprising.

TABLE OF CONTENTS

PART ONE

A New Approach to
Leadership Development

SECTION 1

Playing the Hand You're Dealt

Life is like a game of poker. This thought occurred to me not too long ago as I sat playing a game of cards with my wife and some friends. There was the usual ceremonial griping about the cards being doled out and before the dealer had finished, a couple of the players had already convinced themselves that they had lost the game. They were making comments like, "I can never play this kind of hand right," and "I never get the cards I need." My reaction to this complaining was, *"Just play the hand you're dealt."*

The similarity of the card table conversation that night to coaching conversations I have had with business executives was startling. Struggling with monumental challenges, my courageous clients sometimes grumble about the circumstances they face, the people they work with inside and outside their organizations, and their ability to deal with these circumstances and individuals. They all struggle in their own ways to accept their innate leadership styles.

As a leader, you will be frustrated as well, if you try to change other people or deny the circumstances you face or even your own natural style. Indeed, attempting to make such changes is the source of most frustration. True leadership development begins the

1

moment you accept all three: the people, the circumstances, and particularly your style. In short, *you must play the hand you're dealt.*

Leadership seems to evolve in three stages. At first, leaders ask, "What's wrong with *them?*" (the people they work with). After a time, leaders begin to ask, "What's wrong with *it?*" (their organization, processes, or systems). Eventually, a leader gets around to asking, "What's wrong with *me?* How can I personally improve my performance?" Leadership development requires that you work on all three areas. As a leader, you must be able to interact more effectively with colleagues and co-workers, improve ways of doing work, and change or improve the actions you yourself take. In all cases, the emphasis is on your own performance—not someone else's. In particular, you must begin to put leadership actions into play.

As a successful leader, you most likely are intuitively performing some of the ten leadership initiatives that every successful leader does. Already you are using the ones that come naturally to you. However, understanding all of them, learning the ones that don't come naturally, and doing them intentionally, will accelerate your leadership development.

Practicing all ten leadership initiatives will put leadership at your fingertips and will enable you to focus your energy and that of your organization to create a future full of growth and success. You will learn how to accomplish all this with relative ease by using simple processes and techniques you can easily apply in everyday work situations.

Added to these ten initiatives is the concept of leadership style. You will identify your natural leadership style, determine what kind of leader you are, and confront your strengths and weaknesses. By so doing, you design an action plan for your personal leadership development. You will also learn to accomplish each of the ten leadership initiatives in a manner that suits your natural style.

This book will help you make a clear distinction between managing and leading. The information on leadership will enable you to control your tendency to manage in response to every challenge and request. More importantly, it will allow you to distinguish yourself as a leader within your organization.

The ten leadership initiatives represent the ten actions successful leaders take to ensure the ongoing success of their organization:

- Envisioning—shifts the attention of your organization from the present to the future.

- Managing mindsets—creates a fresh perspective on your products, services, and customers.

- Modeling—keeps you connected to your stakeholders.

- Clarifying values—leverages the most powerful driver of organizational behavior.

- Aligning—makes decisions faster and ensures follow-through.

- Bridging—effectively deals with colleagues and stakeholders who disagree with a team decision or organizational direction.

- Managing breakdowns—removes systemic organizational barriers to cooperation and teamwork.

- Coaching—taps the commitment and energy of individuals within your organization and gets everything people have to give.

- Renewing—creates a new future and thus avoids inevitable decline.

- Acknowledging accomplishment—gives people a sense of fulfillment, which enables them to manage monumental changes.

As you read further in this book, you'll learn:

- What each leadership initiative is and what it accomplishes.
- When to employ each of the ten initiatives.
- How to take specific action using your own natural style.

The ten initiatives represent a series of actions you need to take, at the right time, to keep your organization as a whole moving, growing, and prospering. The absence of any of these initiatives causes an organization to get stuck in a particular phase of development. *The object of the leadership game is the long-term, sustainable growth of your organization.* The ten initiatives put you in that game by enabling you to perform all ten initiatives *using,* rather than changing, your natural leadership style.

The Leadership Your Way Approach

Most books and workshops approach leadership either as *a way to be* or *a set of skills* to be acquired. If you approach leadership development as a way to be or behave, you become an "actor" and your leadership becomes a facade. It's like trying to learn to play poker by acting like a riverboat gambler. Modeling yourself after someone else's ideal, even if it seems to work for a while, takes enormous energy and concentration. When your attention to your behavior lapses, and you revert to your natural style, you may confuse and frustrate those with whom you're working. At best they may feel you are inconsistent, at worst insincere and lacking in genuine leadership ability.

In fact, if you approach leadership only as a set of skills, you are left with the illusion that mastering a skill set allows you to be a leader. At the poker table, memorizing hands, rules, and learning to deal get you into the game, but seldom make you a winner. In the same way, mechanistically applying leadership skills limits your impact. Even if you master these skills and achieve results, you are often left with a lack of fulfillment and little sense of accomplishment.

Accelerated leadership development enables you to:

- Make the most of your own natural style and basic personality—play the hand you're dealt. This book approaches leadership as a set of ten initiatives or mini-processes best accomplished using your own natural style.

- Approach leadership intentionally—rather than just intuitively. You undoubtedly practice some of the ten leadership initiatives automatically and unconsciously. However, practicing them consciously allows you to be consistent. Practicing all ten allows you to address *all* the challenges posed by people and circumstances. This intentional use of leadership initiatives, using your own natural style, is the path to true leadership mastery.

Understanding the ten initiatives and practicing them will help you:

1. Focus organizational energy decisively to achieve desired results.

2. Improve interpersonal relationships, thereby reducing conflicts and stress.

3. Build confidence in your ability to lead.

4. Create the means to ensure the long-term sustainability of your enterprise.

May I deal you in?

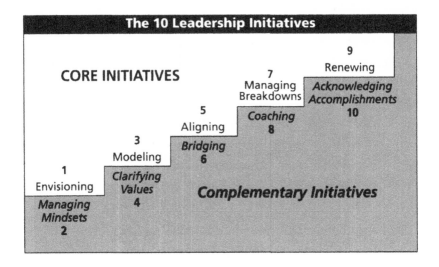

The Ten Leadership Initiatives

You already have everything you need to be a leader. Your current knowledge of the leadership game (your skill, experience, and natural way of operating) has taken you a long way. Learning the ten leadership initiatives will take you the rest of the way.

The ten initiatives form five pairs: five *core* and five *complementary initiatives*. You are probably familiar with most of the core initiatives—envisioning, modeling, aligning, managing breakdowns, and renewing (although you may use different words to describe some of them). However, you may be unaware of the complementary initiatives and their importance.

Complementary initiatives form a foundation and create a context that makes core initiatives more powerful and successful. If you think you're doing everything a leader should be doing and things still aren't working, it's a good bet you're forgetting one or more of the complementary initiatives.

Initiative 1

ENVISIONING creates future-driven action.

Envisioning shifts the attention of your organization from just doing things better, to *doing new things*. With envisioning you can leverage the skills and capabilities of your organization in new ways, so you can retain current customers while attracting new ones, and at the same time keep your most creative workers. Without envisioning, your organization and its people keep doing the same old things, essentially re-creating the past with only slight improvements. Good management creates incremental improvement at best, and that just isn't good enough today. Over time another organization will come along, with a far-reaching bold vision, and steal your customers away and/or provide better service than you, eventually driving you out of business.

Still, good intentions and planning alone don't allow a leadership team or an individual leader to develop a compelling vision that really makes a difference. There are mental barriers that must be dealt with. That's where the complementary initiative to envisioning, managing mindsets, comes into play.

Initiative 2

MANAGING MINDSETS complements Envisioning by allowing your fellow workers and staff to see themselves and your organization from a new, broader, and more powerful perspective.

Managing mindsets reveals the limiting assumptions you and others in your organization hold regarding your products, services, and customers. Examining these mostly hidden assumptions opens the door to previously unseen possibilities for expanding the scope of your business. This initiative contains the power to put your company in an entirely new arena, specifically encouraging each participant to envision a relationship to the company or organization in a new way.

Without managing mindsets, your organization can be blind to problems or opportunities and new possibilities. Ultimately your organization will be unprepared for unforeseen changes and unable to find a lasting competitive advantage. Managing mindsets supports envisioning's focus on doing *new things*.

This complementary initiative brings to the surface never-considered possibilities for leveraging your organization's skills and capabilities. In this way, your vision not only holds more potential, but usually leads to some new product, service, or customer segment that you and your competitors may have overlooked. A compelling vision provides a competitive edge. Think of a vision as selecting the game that you wish to play. Your next step is to assemble and interact with the willing players, which is the focus of the third leadership initiative.

Initiative 3

MODELING provides the bridge connecting your organization to its diverse stakeholders.

Modeling is the process whereby you as a leader personally connect with employees, customers, stockholders, communities, media, and all the other stakeholders in your company, with the intention of addressing their individual needs. By so doing, you give your stakeholders a positive perception of your organization, as well as positive expectations of its future. Modeling must be done on a face-to-face basis, and *you* must do it yourself.

Without a process to integrate everyone's needs, the needs of one or more of your stakeholders will be met at the expense of the other stakeholders. Since meeting the immediate needs of all stakeholders is difficult, the promise of a new and better future for your enterprise allows stakeholders to compromise their short-term needs for their long-term benefit.

The object of modeling is to maintain the commitment of key stakeholders because without it, organizational decline is imminent and inevitable. Modeling forges strong relationships. Its complementary initiative, clarifying values, is the glue that holds these relationships together.

Initiative 4

CLARIFYING VALUES complements Modeling by putting you and the people in your organization in touch with the key elements driving their behavior—their values.

Clarifying values involves identifying your organization's values, with the intention of bringing the other shapers of organizational behavior—vision, mission, strategy, goals, etc.— into alignment with them. Shared values provide a bond that maintains relationships; so clarifying values is a powerful tool for uniting diverse stakeholders.

You may be asking why values are so important to an organization and its leader. Unclear, or poorly articulated values allow your organization to fragment, becoming susceptible to either the whims of persuasive and outspoken managers or marketplace fads. This misdirection squanders resources, making your organization host to an even wider variety of problems. Holding common values, on the other hand, allows your company to balance the needs of your diverse stakeholders. In this way, it serves to support modeling.

Once you've chosen the game, have a vision, and assemble the players or stakeholders, you're ready to deal the cards—to make good decisions.

Initiative 5

ALIGNING unifies a group of people behind a decision and facilitates committed action.

Aligning unites your team or organization behind a specific course of action. This course can best be set once effective, often facilitated, discussions have taken place. Aligning is a decision-making tool that allows you to obtain the benefits of consensus and compromise, without having to deal with the downsides of each. With consensus, decision-making can be an agonizingly long process. Compromise, or a majority rules approach, yields only token acceptance. Alignment generates committed action.

Without alignment, management decisions are often poorly executed and implementation is fraught with problems. The management team that made the initial decision also becomes fragmented and weak, and may even back away from the original decision. Alignment is a powerful tool, but it can be a tricky process to get everyone traveling on the same road. It can work best when coupled with its complementary initiative, bridging.

Initiative 6

BRIDGING complements Aligning by engaging individuals who are in partial or complete disagreement with a decision or direction.

Bridging is really a form of coaching. It's a one-on-one conversation that enables individuals to see ways to meet their personal needs *within* the intended actions of their team. Bridging supports and enables alignment by including any individuals who find themselves unable to *go along* with a team decision.

Without bridging, individual members of your leadership or management team are left out of the decision-making and implementation process. This lack of participation results in a loss of human energy and creativity. Usually it leads to resistance during implementation, a barrier that undermines your effort to achieve a specific objective. Over time, without bridging, your team will settle into a level of mediocre performance characterized by token cooperation and collaboration.

Once you have accomplished these six initiatives, the leadership process is well under way. However, unless you are very lucky, you will encounter problems, or as I prefer to refer to them, breakdowns. Managing breakdowns, the next initiative, begins with identifying and eliminating organizational barriers to cooperation.

Initiative 7

MANAGING BREAKDOWNS creates an organizational context for learning, one that will ultimately keep your organization's action going forward toward your vision.

Managing breakdowns helps you seek out and remove organization-wide barriers to cooperation and teamwork. The objective of this initiative is to make it easier for managers to collaborate and integrate their activities, resulting in an organization which functions as a single team. If you do not proactively manage breakdowns, the dysfunctional organizational behavior that develops around problems will delay action, compromise objectives, and keep your organization in a slow-moving mode of only incremental improvement.

A breakdown is simply a temporary stop in the flow of action. Subjectively, this stop in action is seen as *a problem,* something that "shouldn't be." However, when you form problem-solving teams, or get people to collaborate in problem solving, they have a different relationship to problems. Identifying problems becomes their reason for being. In a context of cooperation, problems become merely breakdowns, or something that "should be," or that is expected in the normal course of work.

Once the context for collaboration and teamwork has been put in place, your organization is positioned to use one of the most powerful tools for individual and organizational development—coaching.

Initiative 8

COACHING complements Managing Breakdowns by improving people's confidence in their ability to perform or by putting and keeping these people in action.

Coaching enables individuals, who are unable or unwilling to continue working toward an objective to: assess the *breakdown* objectively; develop new, previously unseen possibilities for action; and commit to a specific action or actions. Coaching allows individuals to take personal advantage of the cooperative environment that has been created by the managing breakdowns initiative.

Unfortunately leaders and organizations often substitute control for coaching, using negative reinforcement to keep action going in the face of breakdowns. This approach is counterproductive. Using control decreases discretionary productivity and morale. It doesn't take long for individuals to mentally "check out" of the organization. Coaching, however, keeps action going without using direct or indirect threats and fear. It bolsters the human spirit, builds morale, and sustains positive organizational growth—but not forever.

Ironically, within your success the seeds for your demise are sown. For any number of reasons your enterprise will eventually find itself at the end of its life cycle, a reality which brings us to the last two leadership initiatives.

Initiative 9

RENEWING involves starting the leadership process all over again—beginning with Envisioning—at just the right time.

Renewing is the process of beginning a *new* business or phase of your business using the assets of your existing organization capital, competencies, human resources, existing customers, and market position. In most cases renewing involves "tearing down" all or part of your existing organizational structure, redesigning processes, and acquiring new knowledge and skills.

The trick to knowing when the time is right for renewing will be discussed in detail in Part Two. For now, it is enough to say that sustainable growth requires a cycle of periodic renewal. Without renewal an organization will stagnate and decline or else leave itself open to external forces of change, which are more difficult to manage. Most, if not all, leaders recognize the importance of renewal. However, most are unaware of the relationship of the next initiative, acknowledging accomplishment, to renewal.

Initiative 10

ACKNOWLEDGING ACCOMPLISHMENT gives your stakeholders a genuine sense of accomplishment and personal fulfillment with regard to their contributions to your organization.

By acknowledging accomplishment, you get everyone in your organization looking back to see how far your enterprise has come and how they have personally contributed to its success. Acknowledging accomplishment allows people to be successful and to feel fulfilled.

If accomplishment is not acknowledged, individuals find it difficult to engage in renewal. Even if they do, they will not bring the same level of commitment to a new vision as they would have if their previous contribution had been acknowledged. Over time

13

a lack of acknowledgment leads to a decrease in human energy and morale, and inevitably to decline.

Acknowledging accomplishment complements renewal because without it, people may tend to see the dramatic changes created by the renewing initiative—the reorganizations, reengineering, and other dramatic changes—as indications that their past contributions have not been needed, valued, or appreciated. Acknowledging accomplishment gets at one of the primary reasons people go to work—the feeling that they are making a valuable contribution to their community and the world. While acknowledging accomplishment is the last of the ten initiatives, it provides the impetus for beginning again, with yet another vision.

In Part Two of this book we will explore each of the ten leadership initiatives: their purpose, indicators that they are needed, the process of each initiative, and personal coaching based upon your natural ability to perform each initiative. While you will want to explore all ten initiatives, it makes sense to focus on those that are particularly troublesome. Bringing your innate leadership style and natural abilities into the game allows you to play at a new, more powerful level. It's your *ace in the hole.*

SECTION 2

Playing the Cards You're Dealt

The leadership game is like draw poker. You're dealt five cards and you can discard three of them. Some of the cards that life deals you include educational opportunities, economic status, cultural norms, and traumatic experiences. If these work against you, you can change them with hard work and persistence. Others like gender, physical handicaps, and ethnic background, of course, cannot be discarded, but can be transcended if they cause your problems. However, there is one card that you cannot discard—your basic style or temperament.

You were born with certain tendencies that never change. These tendencies and preferences have an impact on every aspect of your life, especially your work life. Some tendencies contribute to your natural leadership ability; others make leadership more difficult. You can't discard your leadership style, but you can turn it to your advantage. In effect, leadership style becomes a wild card, making the hand you hold better and the odds of winning greater. Becoming aware of your natural ways of doing things, your leadership style, is the first step on your journey to leadership mastery.

Defining Personal Leadership Style

Personal style is something you're born with. Since the beginning of recorded history, men have noted distinct differences in people's dispositions and surmised that there were different types of people. The Greek physician Hippocrates described four human attributes he called *humors*. More recently Swiss psychologist Carl Jung identified four personality dimensions he labeled *sensing, feeling, thinking,* and *intuitive.* Jung's work formed the foundation for a variety of useful personal style assessments, the most commonly used one being the Myers-Briggs Type Indicator. While there are many different labels and approaches to describing personality type or temperament, most identify four basic dimensions or attributes. So it is with leadership style.

The Four Styles

You have a leadership style composed of a blend of four dimensions, but you are predominantly influenced by one of the four. My own research and experience with organizational leaders have provided me with the basis to come up with my own definition of leadership styles. I have defined the four as the **Commander,** the **Strategist,** the **Coach,** and the **Performer.** Knowing which type of leader you are gives you an edge in leadership development because:

- You can accelerate your development by focusing on those areas that need improvement, not wasting time on things you naturally do well.

- You can become aware of natural tendencies and behaviors that get in the way or cause problems, so you can modify your behavior to avoid such difficulties.

- You can put each of the ten leadership initiatives into action in a natural manner, reducing stress and giving yourself a genuine sense of fulfillment.

Determining Your Style

This book will be more meaningful and useful if you can identify your predominant leadership style, the one that best describes your overall behavior. There are many instruments designed to help you zero in on your unique personal style. Among the most popular of these are simple self-assessment tools like the Myers-Briggs Type Indicator and CRG's Personal Style Indicator (PSI). There are also more detailed, often computer-scored instruments, such as HRDQ, DiSC, and the Birkman Method. Keep in mind that each assessment uses different terms, or labels, to describe the four basic styles; so you must do some "translation" to use them with this book. All instruments and inventories gather information about how you prefer to act and the way you see yourself and the world. They determine your precise personal style and mix of the four dimensions. However, simply knowing your own predominant style dimension is all that you need to make good use of this book.

In place of a complex style-assessment instrument, you can simply answer three questions that I often ask a client in an initial coaching session. Your answers will indicate your predominant leadership style and even provide a hint of your secondary style dimensions.

LEADERSHIP STYLE ASSESSMENT

INSTRUCTIONS: Put a **2** in the box next to the answer which is **MOST like you.** Put a **1** next to any answer which is **SOMEWHAT like you:**

1. While I have many attributes or characteristics, taken as a group, the three that describe me **BEST** are:

Description	Symbol
Competitive, decisive, and direct	♦
Influential, impulsive, and fun	♠
Supportive, reliable, and adaptable	♥
Knowledgeable, careful, and organized	♣

2. In evaluating whether or not to take a new job or assignment, I tend to look for:

Description	Symbol
A workplace where knowledge, quality, and accuracy are valued and where there is some degree of stability.	♣
A fast-moving environment that offers variety and is one where people will notice, need, and appreciate my creative talents.	♠
An organization where people work together, get along, and where human needs are balanced with achieving beneficial results.	♥
A position in which I have a high degree of control and where there are significant financial rewards and the ability to advance quickly.	♦

3. My behaviors that most often lead to problems with other people are:

	Description	Symbol
☐	My willingness to include everyone, and my easygoing manner, which often leads to others ignoring my needs.	♥
☐	My decisiveness and need to keep the process moving, which others often see as domineering and controlling.	♦
☐	My highly verbal, outgoing manner, which others sometimes perceive as my "stealing the show" or monopolizing the conversation.	♠
☐	My need for quality and accuracy, a trait which others often see as being critical or finicky.	♣

Note the playing card icons next to each of your answers and add up the number of points for each of the four suits. Please place the totals in the box next to each icon. The suit with the highest number of points indicates your predominant leadership style—as follows:

SCORING

POINTS	SYMBOL	DESCRIPTION
☐	♦	The Commander
☐	♣	The Strategist
☐	♥	The Coach
☐	♠	The Performer

19

In addition to identifying your predominant leadership style (the one with the most points), you should make note of any suit where you scored three or more points. This secondary dimension also influences your style, but to a lesser degree. If you happen to have a tie—two suits or dimensions with the same number of points, you are a blend of both of those styles.

To help you further zero in on your leadership style, look over the following profiles to see if the style indicated in the above assessment "suits" you. You may also want to read the description of your secondary dimension (where you scored three or more points). If you had a tie between two equally strong style dimensions, you will want to read both profiles and mentally blend them together.

♦ If you are a **Commander**, you like to be in control. You are on the go—an action-oriented, high-energy person. You eagerly take on new, often risky, challenges. You are quick to set goals and make plans and prefer to work alone since others only seem to hold you back or slow you down. You tend to work long, hard hours. You almost always achieve the goals you set for yourself and are generally viewed as successful.

♣ If you are a **Strategist**, you are an expert at analysis and problem solving. You tend to think things through slowly and carefully, questioning and evaluating nearly everything and everyone. You like people, but not large groups or gatherings. You can be outspoken, but only if you've studied all the facts and are confident of your information. You like to give advice and may often do so in one-on-one situations.

♥ If you are a **Coach**, everyone seems to like you, and you want to keep it that way. You are extremely helpful and caring, sometimes to a fault. You like to work in team settings and you make sure everyone on the team has an opportunity to participate. While you like people, you are generally reserved in the way you relate to others and don't like show-boating.

♠ If you are a **Performer**, you are the classic party animal. You enjoy talking with anyone about anything. You are entertaining, a trait which serves you well, as you are also very persuasive. Many see you as the "creative type." You most likely engage in artistic activities professionally or recreationally (writing, painting, cooking, dancing, photography, decorating, etc.). People like being around you because you are fun and you're comfortable being in the middle of it all.

Now that you've completed your assessment and reviewed the characteristics of the four types, you are beginning to consider what style you have, and the kind of hand you've been dealt. Approaching leadership development without knowing your predominant style is like trying to play poker without knowing your "hole card" (the one dealt face down). You can still put together a winning hand using the four cards showing, but your odds of winning go up dramatically when you include that fifth card. Knowing and leveraging your own style—that "fifth card"—make leadership *your* way possible.

Leadership Your Way Is the Only Way

One of my first coaching clients, Barbara, was a prime candidate for the leadership your way approach. Indeed, I have not known many people who focused on leadership development with the intensity that Barbara did. Being one of only a handful of women to break through the glass ceiling, Barbara had an office on the top floor at the headquarters of one of the largest accounting firms in the country. As I entered her office for our first meeting, I noticed she had nearly every business best seller on her bookshelf, which also held various professional and personal awards.

Barbara began our meeting even before I had a chance to sit down. "I've read your literature and your promise of results. That's what I want—results! Tell me how you can help me."

I felt like I was dealing with an individual with a Commander style, so I got right to the point. "I work through a series of in-depth discussions in which we explore the actions you take as leader, what triggers those actions, and the short- and long-term effects of your behavior."

Before I had a chance to continue, Barbara interrupted. "My behavior? Look, I don't need a therapist."

"Coaching isn't therapy," I replied. "Although individuals often come to understand the motivations for their actions, the focus is on changing behavior in a way that's compatible with your style."

"There's only one style that works around here," Barbara replied. It became clear that she believed a hard-nosed, intimidating style was necessary to be a leader, particularly since she was a woman. But this was *not* Barbara's natural style.

While Barbara was successful by many standards, it seemed she was unhappy and concerned that she wouldn't be able to keep the facade in place much longer. Her dilemma was not unusual for executives. Many people associate leadership with a commanding and controlling type of behavior, but personal and professional accomplishments are not reserved for Commander-style leaders only. The style that will work best for you—your own leadership style—is the only one that will give you long-term success and happiness. **There is no one style that is better suited to leadership than another.**

Understanding how the ten leadership initiatives relate to your dominant leadership style will give you *table stakes* to get into the leadership game. Your dominant style reveals innate strengths that allow you to excel in some areas of leadership. You also have tendencies and preferred ways of acting that make some of the leadership initiatives more difficult to pull off. The profiles that follow will illustrate how your style translates into natural leadership ability (the pluses). They will also point out those tendencies that can cause problems if they are not managed (the minuses).

LEADERSHIP PLUSES & MINUSES

Read the profile for your dominant style dimension. You may also want to glance at the profile of any secondary dimension. The pluses (+) represent your natural strengths. The minuses (−) call attention to areas that may cause you difficulty.

Commander

Leadership Profile

✚ If you're a Commander-type leader, you're a high-energy, action-oriented person. Straightforward and direct, willing and eager to make decisions, you take responsibility and do whatever is necessary to reach your objective. No one wants to be standing between you and your goal. Still, while you can be intimidating, you are also an honest person, a visionary, and an excellent negotiator.

▬ As a Commander, you prefer to work alone. When working with others, you often leave them behind if they move too slowly. You can be judgmental. Your need to feel and be in control is the cause of much frustration and stress. In addition, your tendency to be abrupt and domineering puts unnecessary stress on personal relationships.

Strategist

Leadership Profile

- ✚ The calm methodical diplomat comes to mind when describing you as the Strategist-leader. Extremely perceptive, you get all the facts before making a decision and are an expert at analyzing data and information. You are fair and unbiased—a clear, accurate communicator. No one has to guess what you mean when you speak. You say exactly what you mean in a well-structured way. Indeed, everything you do is structured.
- ▬ Your thoroughness may tend to become perfectionism. You hate to make mistakes. For that reason, you take time, perhaps too much time, to make decisions and are often seen as indecisive. You will take calculated risks, but only after an almost agonizing analysis. Strategist-leaders don't like change and will tend to avoid making changes. This reluctance to make adjustments can lead to an inability to make timely decisions.

Coach

Leadership Profile

✛ As a Coach-type leader, you often lead from behind the scenes. You are warm, likable, faithful, and unselfish—the kinder and gentler leader. Known as a team player, you are understanding, willing, and eager to listen and, for that reason, provide excellent coaching and counseling. You care about people and they tend to know it. During a conflict, you're usually the peacemaker. Your ability to stay calm in a crisis, along with your open and honest manner, makes you an excellent facilitator.

▭ Your nonassertive nature, while helpful in one regard, can cause you to sublimate your own needs. You tend to give highest priority to people issues, sometimes ignoring pressing business needs. When corrective action is called for, you are sometimes slow to deal with difficult situations. You like to maintain harmony, occasionally at great cost to yourself or your team. This characteristic may prompt you to avoid risky situations and maintain the status quo, which is a tendency leaders can't afford.

Performer

Leadership Profile

♣ As a Performer you're always on the move. Exciting and enthusiastic, you like to put a bit of fun into everything you do. You're an excellent communicator. Combined with your friendly and sociable style, you can also be very persuasive. While you have strong opinions, you are generally open-minded and flexible. Your natural intuitive ability and compassion allow you to connect with people very quickly, and often on a deep level. You're the proverbial stranger on a bus whom everyone confides in.

▬ While good at creating new programs and initiatives, you often lose interest after the start-up. This lack of follow-up often sends mixed messages to those trying to implement programs. Easily bored and sometimes undisciplined, you can rush from one thing to the next and often find yourself over-committed. In meetings, your natural tendency to take over and dominate can hurt others' feelings. It can sometimes even cut you off from valuable feedback from colleagues.

As you can see, no one style embodies an ideal leader—each has its pluses and minuses. Winning in the leadership game depends less on the cards you've been dealt, and more on how you play them. Your leadership style makes some of the ten leadership initiatives natural for you. Other tendencies might cause you to avoid certain initiatives. Knowing those leadership initiatives that you may tend to avoid or undervalue will provide the key to dramatic leadership development.

Using the Natural Ability Index

As you begin to practice each leadership initiative, you will realize that some come easily to you while others do not—primarily due to your leadership style. You'll want to concentrate on those initiatives that need development, because if they're causing you problems, they're probably causing your organization problems too.

To help you identify which of the initiatives might be more difficult for you, a Natural Ability Index is included within the Natural Ability section for each of the ten initiatives. This index is a one-to-ten numerical rating that quantifies your natural ability for a particular initiative. It is an instrument I developed based upon years of coaching experiences. The Natural Ability Index will be explained in more detail at the start of Part Two, just before you begin exploring the ten leadership initiatives.

The Leadership Process

If you're like most leaders, you have risen through the ranks based upon your management ability. You get things done. It's only natural for you, as a leader, to continue doing what has made you successful. But that tendency to *manage* can take you out of the leadership game unless you learn the difference between the two—unless you learn when to lead and when to manage.

> **Leadership focuses on *where to go* and *what to do*.**
> **Management focuses on *how to get there* and *how to do it better*.**

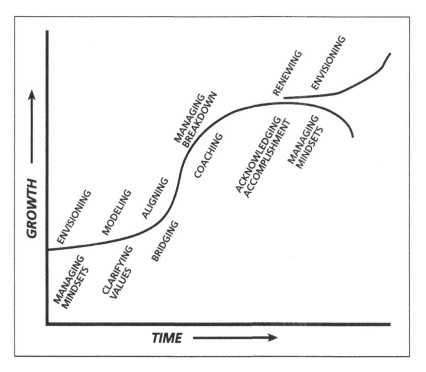

Leadership Growth Cycle

Understanding and practicing the ten leadership initiatives will enable you to distinguish leadership from management. Taken in turn, the ten form an overall leadership process flowing from envisioning through renewing. Repeated frequently, this leadership process creates a familiar growth cycle. It is this continuous process, the consistent application of leadership initiatives, that results in sustainable growth for an organization.

As this leadership-growth cycle suggests, each of the leadership initiatives is associated with a particular phase of development in your organization's overall growth cycle. The absence of any of these acts will cause your organization to experience problems, or get hung up in a particular phase of development. Putting all of the ten initiatives into play keeps your organization moving, forward and upward. Furthermore, the ease and speed with which you can move through this cycle, and go on to repeat it again and again, determine your real leadership effectiveness.

The ten-act leadership process, combined with an understanding and appreciation of leadership style, offers a new and effective way to approach leadership development. As you explore each of the ten initiatives and reflect on the personal coaching geared to your unique style, you will be able to immediately begin applying what you learn in your daily work. Leadership will change from a vague concept to a natural way of being. Putting the ten initiatives into play will put you in the leadership game and keep your organization growing and prospering.

Ante up!

PART TWO

The Initiatives in Action

APPROACHING THE INITIATIVES
A Four-Part Structure

In this section of *Leadership Your Way,* each of the ten leadership initiatives will be explored using the same four-part structured approach. Following this consistent format, you will be able to easily grasp, compare, connect, and contrast the ten initiatives.

Much as you would learn a card game, you'll learn the object of each leadership initiative, why you perform each one, and what it buys you. You'll move on to the basics, including identifying when a particular initiative is needed, and the process for performing each initiative. Finally, you'll get coaching tips that show you how to leverage your natural ability. Here is the four-part structure used to explain the ten leadership initiatives.

The PURPOSE

The PURPOSE section tells you why you would want to perform each initiative, what you gain by doing it, and what you risk by not doing it.

To change anything, especially your behavior, it's necessary to *want* to change. The PURPOSE sections help you weigh benefits and costs, so you can choose whether to change your behavior or not.

The INDICATORS

The INDICATORS section points to specific events, behaviors, actions, and results that may indicate a leadership initiative is needed.

When you see these indicators, take action! Many indicators are given for each leadership initiative. The presence of several indicators suggests an increased likelihood an initiative is called for, or how much demand there is for it.

Indicators are a diagnostic tool. They point to apparent problems. If you approach these problems from a management perspective, you'll likely go into a problem-solving mode and primarily address the symptoms. The INDICATORS section allows you to approach problems and situations from a *leadership* perspective, so you will address the deep, underlying cause and make changes in organizational structure, processes, and systems so that "the problem" doesn't appear again in another form.

The PROCESS

The PROCESS section gives you the basic elements that make up each leadership initiative. In many cases, you'll get a step-by-step process.

The PROCESS section quickly gets you to take action. What's more important, knowing the process for putting an initiative into play allows you to do it over and over again *consistently*. Intuitive leadership behavior works much of the time. *Intentional* leadership behavior works *all* of the time.

Whether you get basic elements or a detailed step-by-step method in the PROCESS section, the information is given in a way that allows you to put each initiative into play by using your natural leadership style. You are told *what* needs to be done, but not *how* to do it. That comes in the NATURAL ABILITY section, which offers you specific tips and coaching based on the type of leader you are.

Your NATURAL ABILITY

The NATURAL ABILITY section gives you specific coaching tips, suggestions, and advice on how you can approach action in a manner that's consistent with your natural style.

This not only allows you to put the initiatives into play, but to do so in a manner that's natural and comfortable for you. Consequently, you will show up as an authentic leader. But, the most valuable benefit of knowing your natural leadership abilities is that it allows you to pinpoint the initiatives that need improvement and build on ones that are already strong.

To help you identify which of the initiatives might be more difficult for you, a Natural Ability Index has been added within the Natural Ability sections. The Natural Ability Index is a one-to-ten rating that ranks your natural ability for each of the ten initiatives. By identifying the three or four initiatives which are more difficult for you, it is possible to create your own personal leadership development plan.

The Natural Ability Index works like this: a high number means that an initiative comes naturally to you; a low number suggests you may have some difficulty using the initiative or putting it into action. For each leadership style, the index number appears as follows:

♣ Managing Mindsets for the STRATEGIST

Natural Ability Index: 10

On a scale of one to ten:

* A rating of one to three indicates you do not value or practice the initiative; it's one that is difficult for you, or that you may undervalue or totally overlook.

- A rating of four to seven indicates you have a moderate natural ability to perform the initiative. You have both negative and positive tendencies with regard to this initiative. It is likely that you probably perform it inconsistently, with varying degrees of success.

- A rating of eight to ten indicates that you probably practice this initiative intuitively. It comes naturally to you. Indeed, it is your approach to these high-scoring initiatives that has made you successful. You can become even more masterful with additional coaching and practice.

I developed the Natural Ability Index chart after years of coaching leaders and hundreds of coaching sessions. In essence, the leaders whom I was coaching helped develop the Natural Ability Index. Most introductory coaching sessions included a quick review of the ten leadership initiatives followed by a simple question, "Which initiatives are you forgetting or performing poorly?" The leaders' collective answers, combined with first-hand observations, determined which initiatives each of the four types of leaders did well, and which initiatives they did poorly or not at all.

The Natural Ability Index chart can help you identify the three or four leadership initiatives that will likely cause you the most trouble, those with a low rating. While you will want to pay particular attention to those low-scoring initiatives, you need to strike a balance and practice all ten. After you are familiar with all ten initiatives, you may wish to come back to this chart to develop a comprehensive self-development plan, intentionally putting each of the ten initiatives to work in your organization one by one, beginning with the ones that pose the greatest challenge for you.

Natural Ability Index

The Four Leadership Styles

The Ten Leadership Initiatives	Commander	Strategist	Coach	Performer
Envisioning	8	9	4	9
Managing Mindsets	3	10	7	5
Modeling	9	1	3	10
Clarifying Values	4	8	9	3
Aligning	7	4	6	6
Bridging	5	6	5	7
Managing Breakdowns	6	7	2	1
Coaching	1	5	10	2
Renewing	10	2	1	8
Acknowledging Accomplishment	2	3	8	4

INITIATIVE 1: ENVISIONING
Creating Future-Driven Action

One way to look at envisioning is to conjure up a picture of an archer, a bow and arrow, and a target. The bull's eye in the target represents the *vision* of your organization, and the bow and arrow are the *strategic and operating plans* of that group.

This model shows the relationship of vision, mission, and strategic plan to the people in your organization. A leader doesn't hold the bow; the employees do. As leader, you put the target in place and paint the bull's-eye in the middle, telling people *exactly* where to aim—where to focus their attention, energy, and resources. Envisioning is one of the clearest manifestations of your leadership because it literally puts you in front of the organization, providing direction and motivation. While this one initiative alone will not ensure continued growth and viability, it is the place where leadership begins.

PURPOSE of Envisioning

Envisioning is the initiative that invents a new, well-defined, and specific future for your enterprise. It sets a mark you want to hit in about five years' time. To understand how a vision works and why

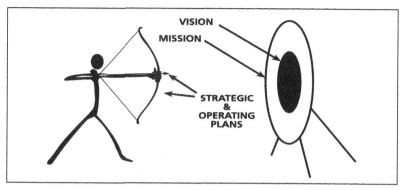

Vision, Mission & Strategic Plans

it's important to an organization, you need to take a good look at human nature.

Most of your decision-making is instinctive and automatic. However, all of your actions have thought processes behind them. You evaluate a situation, identify possible actions, choose one, and finally act. You make thousands of such decisions every day, but what goes on during this process is often a mystery because it happens so quickly. For example, when a colleague sticks his head in your office to ask if you want to go to lunch, you usually respond immediately. In the two or three seconds between, "Want to go to lunch?" and your answer, there's an automatic and "invisible" thought process. This subconscious process is the way we make most decisions, including those in business.

For example, if a new marketing survey made you aware of a growing customer need that suggested a new product or service that falls outside your company's traditional product line, would you as a leader encourage your organization to pursue the development of that product? Although this business decision might suggest a thorough and methodical decision-making process, you'd likely make the call in an instant. But during that instant almost unconscious decision-making takes place.

Subconsciously, the thought of pioneering a radical new product conjures up instantaneous "snapshot memories" . . . possibly of the last new product that failed. You might recall colleagues whose careers took some turns for the worse when they unsuccessfully took on the chief financial officer to launch a new product. Given those events, you would not choose to champion a new product. However, if your subconscious "snapshot memories" were more pleasant, you would be inclined to propose the new product. The point is simply that most of your decisions and actions are instantaneous and based upon *past history*.

Actions driven by *past experience* are comfortable. They provide a feeling of safety because they maintain the status quo. Unfortunately, decisions based upon *past history* don't create quantum leaps in performance or ensure long-term growth. Dramatic change and growth happen when actions are driven by a new, future possibility. If, instead of recalling past events, you focus on what that new product might mean to the company and your career (how it might generate an entirely new revenue stream, how it might be a way for you to demonstrate your leadership ability, etc.), you would not only decide to champion the new product, but you would take quick, decisive, and powerful action. Envisioning results in actions driven by a *future possibility*, rather than *past experience*.

Envisioning is an important act because, without it, human beings and organizations only create more of what already exists, making it slightly better or somewhat different. While that may have been adequate 10 or 20 years ago, incremental improvements are bound to fail in today's rapidly evolving world. As it was put so poignantly in the Old Testament Book of Proverbs, "Where there is no vision, the people perish." So do organizations.

How do you know if envisioning is missing from your organization? What are the "telltale signs" that indicate envisioning is called for? A quick check of the indicators below answers both questions.

INDICATORS That Envisioning Is Needed

Knowing when to put envisioning into play is just as important as knowing how to create a vision. Fortunately distinct circumstances and events tell you if and when to act. If you can put a check by three or more of the following indicators, envisioning is needed in your organization:

❑ Stagnating or declining stock price in spite of good overall organizational performance and respectable dividends.

❑ A downward trend in market share for two years or more.

❑ Strategic planning that is primarily a budgeting process and/or most strategic objectives are financial targets.

❑ Constant strategy shifting—significant changes in strategy announced two or more times in a 12-month period.

❑ Functional or operational units within the enterprise consistently meet their annual objectives and yet the overall organizational performance is not improving.

❑ No significant product or service developments or innovations in a 12-month period.

❑ Decreasing individual (not necessarily overall organizational) productivity.

❑ Employee survey results in which more than one-half of the respondents indicate that the direction of the organization is unknown or unclear. (Warning: This can be the result of other missing leadership initiatives—i.e., aligning, bridging, etc.)

No single indicator should trigger the envisioning initiative, but the presence of three or more would give you reason to suspect envisioning is needed, even if your enterprise has a vision statement. Indeed, it's not uncommon to find organizations, with a vision statement on every bulletin board, still crying out for envisioning. The presence of a vision does not negate the possibility that the envisioning initiative is needed.

While most organizations are able to see envisioning as a leadership initiative, the process and results often fall short of what is needed to change organizational behavior. A semiannual corporate "vision quest" is oftentimes an empty ritual characterized by a low-energy meeting punctuated with high-energy rounds of golf. Anyone involved with such a process will tell you that a new or revitalized vision is rarely created. This happens because the vision not only lacks key elements, but the envisioning *process* is missing some critical elements as well.

The Envisioning PROCESS

A common difficulty encountered in the envisioning process is a lack of agreement over the definition of a vision. Specifically, a vision reveals *exactly* where a company is going—the bull's-eye on the target. The vision is different from the mission, which is the entire target. The mission describes the business you're in: the products and services you provide, your service area, your customers, and possibly your competitive advantage. With that in mind, a *vision* for Acme Computer might be: Acme will double its overall market share in the next five years by expanding it's product line to include, and being first to market with, low-cost small business solutions. The *mission* for Acme might be: Acme provides the lowest cost operations management software and on-site support to enterprises operating within North America.

Initiating a successful envisioning process requires three critical success factors:

1. The process used to create the vision statement should take into account your leadership style and that of the individuals helping you create the vision statement.

2. Secondly, the vision statement itself should meet four criteria to be effective.

3. Finally, the vision must be linked to day-to-day operations.

Let's explore each of these success factors in more detail.

1. **The envisioning process should take into account your leadership style and that of the others who are co-authoring the vision—typically your management team.** The envisioning initiative comes naturally to you if you are a Strategist, Performer, or Commander; however the process used to create and implement the vision will differ. The Strategist would best be served by a highly structured process. The Performer would probably prefer an interpersonal approach that includes extensive discussions. The Commander would like high-energy meetings in which individuals and their ideas "duke it out." However, envisioning comes less naturally to the Coach. The Coach would benefit from a facilitated process, probably one which would include everyone's vision. No matter what your leadership style, once you have designed a process compatible with your own style and those of your colleagues, you can turn your attention to the vision statement itself.

2. As you, and those co-authoring the vision statement, go to work, keep in mind the second success factor—**that the final vision statement should meet four specific criteria.** Indeed, unless it meets these four important criteria, it is unlikely your

vision will be able to influence people in your organization or change organizational behavior. Your vision statement should:

- Be specific in time—planned for about five years ahead.
- Be clear—promising a measurable bottom-line result.
- Be compelling—challenging and exciting.
- Paradoxically, be a "stretch," yet seem plausible or possible.

If the time frame is planned for only two to three years ahead, stretch targets—objectives which are far beyond business-as-usual—seem impossible. People in your organization won't take the vision seriously or they'll give up before they even begin. If the vision is too far out, say seven to ten years, it won't stimulate immediate, near-term changes.

If the vision is too vague, it will not be easy to link strategic and operating plans to it. For example, one of my clients, a vice-president for marketing and sales, worked for a company whose vision read, "We will be among the top ten software development companies in the U.S." What do you think this VP did in response to that vision? Nothing . . . at least nothing more than he was already doing. This vision statement was not only vague and unclear, but far from compelling. It's difficult to get excited about being in the top ten. A vision must strike a delicate balance between being a compelling stretch and seeming doable.

If your vision statement meets these four criteria, it will shift the drivers of organizational behavior to a future orientation. Without such a forward-looking vision, your organization will ultimately lose both its customers and its competitive position.

But, what if your vision is slightly off target? It is far riskier *not* to have a vision, than it is to have one that is slightly imperfect or off the mark. Indeed, any vision with stretch objectives will undoubtedly be slightly off the mark because it makes demands on people and organizations that stretch them far beyond business-as-usual results. For that reason, visions can and should be revisited and adjusted every year or two to account for changing circumstances. The greatest purpose of a vision is that it be a *catalyst for action*, leading to long-term growth. Of course, a proper vision *alone* is no guarantee of future-driven action. You need one additional element.

3. Your envisioning process should not end with the drafting of the vision statement. **The third and final critical success factor for envisioning requires that you find ways to translate the vision into discrete strategic activities and ultimately into annual operations plans and the budgeting process.** This highly structured vision-management process is a critical part of the envisioning initiative. Putting the vision into action requires the practice of other leadership initiatives as well.

As you will recall, the first critical success factor requires that you develop an envisioning process that is compatible with *your* leadership style. The Natural Ability section that follows gives you specific coaching tips, suggestions, and advice on how to design and implement an envisioning process that suits your natural way of doing things.

Your NATURAL ABILITY for Envisioning

It's not only *easier* to carry out a leadership initiative by using your natural style, but doing so also allows you to operate in a consistent manner. There are four sections—one for each dominant leadership style, Commander, Strategist, Coach, or Performer—within each Natural Ability section. You should focus on one of them—*your* dominant leadership style, as identified in Part One. First, read the coaching tips offered for your particular leadership style, then scan the other coaching sections, as they will give you insights into the behavior of your colleagues.

The Natural Ability Index number, which precedes each coaching section, indicates among other factors, the degree of difficulty a particular leadership initiative represents for you. If your index number for envisioning is 7 or higher, then envisioning is relatively easy for you. If your index number is 3 or lower, you may have some difficulty with it. A Natural Ability Index of 4, 5, or 6, suggests you have modest ability, but may need further development. But whatever your ranking, you can always improve your performance. Just read the coaching tips for your style in the next few pages and improve your ability to put envisioning into play.

◆ Envisioning for the COMMANDER

Natural Ability Index: 8

As a Commander you epitomize the statement, *I'd rather do it myself* when you approach most tasks. When it comes to envisioning, you tend to consider the leadership initiatives as your sole responsibility. Resist this tendency. A vision works best when it's *shared*, so you need to foster participation by others.

Here is an example. Once you decide to set a new organizational vision, a declaration at your next staff meeting that a new vision is needed would not be out of order; nevertheless, it would be a welcome surprise if your declaration were followed by a sincere request for suggestions and feedback from colleagues throughout the process. You might suggest a series of concise strategic briefings, led by various team members, to lay the foundation for a new vision. Of course, there's nothing wrong with drafting the vision alone; indeed it has elements of control as well as drama and spectacle, which you enjoy. However, if you go this route, remember to receive and acknowledge team input along the way. Once the vision statement is finalized, use your commanding presence to communicate the vision personally to stakeholders. In terms of follow-through, you intuitively find ways to tie planning and budgeting to the vision objectives. Holding people's feet to the fire comes naturally to you. With your lead, vision objectives are easily accomplished, especially if you've found a palatable way to include others in the act.

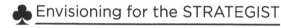 Envisioning for the STRATEGIST

Natural Ability Index: 9

The statement, "Let's think this through," is the Strategist's approach to most challenges, so the envisioning process could become lengthy. That's not all bad if you build in status reports and continuous organizational communication along the way. But, as you may be aware, people often incorrectly interpret your lengthy decision-making process as a lack of resolve or commitment on your part. This same misconception can also be true as you approach the envisioning initiative.

A well-structured and thorough envisioning process will work best for you, particularly with regard to the initial strategic assessment. For you, participation is best accomplished through a series of small group meetings. It would be natural to request respected and trusted individuals to submit drafts of their own visions. Making it known that you will consider their input seriously will help satisfy their need to be included. Eventually, you will successfully homogenize all the feedback and data into one clear, concise vision statement. And, while you, as a Strategist, don't often team up with Performers, the final vision statement may need stylish touches that a Performer would add.

You'll not likely want to take the final vision on the road personally, but you need to be closely identified with it. Perhaps you could communicate the new vision via videotape or a printed interview with pictures. This would satisfy your need to get the words just right and still provide a comfortable way for you to demonstrate your commitment to the new vision.

Once the vision is in place, managing a process for tracking progress will come easily for you, but don't go overboard. Don't burden the organization with time-consuming and complex data gathering and reporting. Most people need less data than you do to feel comfortable—and most organizations can't afford extensive tracking processes and systems. Your biggest leadership challenge is to overcome your discomfort over having to make quick decisions with only a moderate amount of data and information.

♥ Envisioning for the COACH

Natural Ability Index: 4

If you are a Coach, the statement *"What do you think the vision should be?"* will be on your lips at the start of the envisioning process. Allowing everyone to participate comes naturally to you. If anything, you might even tend to allow more discussion and feedback than necessary. A facilitator to lead the initial strategic assessment and drafting process might be helpful to keep the process moving.

As you move through the envisioning process, there also will be conflict and disagreement along the way, another good reason to have a facilitator. However, some disagreement is healthy, and in those darker moments when conflicts arise, remember that the primary value of a vision is its ability to generate future action. Getting alignment on the exact direction is less important than getting everyone moving in the same direction.

As you roll out the vision, you will likely want it to be presented as a team effort. For instance, including the signatures of the executive team members under the vision statement is a popular way to demonstrate that the envisioning process was a team effort. However, you need to focus on accountability and follow-through, not just communication. As a Coach you often tend to cut people too much slack. Design a tough but fair monitoring process that links the operating plans of your teammates to the ultimate accomplishment of the vision. Then let that process itself maintain accountability, so you won't have to use a lot of personal pressure. Finally, don't be so quick to accept excuses if teammates miss interim objectives. Not accomplishing something with a good excuse is not the same as accomplishing it, particularly when it comes to envisioning. Keep to the schedule of the interim goals you set out.

Envisioning for the PERFORMER

Natural Ability Index: 9

The envisioning initiative involves some flair and spectacle that naturally appeals to you. As a Performer, you'll undoubtedly be among the first to see the need for envisioning. In addition, you'll be tempted to *lead* your team's effort to develop a vision; however, it may be advisable for someone else to introduce the process. As you will come to understand, leaders don't always lead from in front.

You may, as a Performer, have already established a reputation for promoting the latest management process or fad. If so, the envisioning process may be a tough sell because of the way others see you. Maybe you should use your persuasive powers to get colleagues to plant the seeds, and let them bring up the subject. But heed one warning. Since you are comfortable operating with little or no structure, the envisioning process can become a three-ring circus if you're not careful. A Strategist or Coach style leader on the team would love to design a structured envisioning process, so let him or her do it.

The participation in the creation of the vision presents few problems for you, but including others in the process afterwards may be more difficult. When it comes time to communicate the vision to the organization at large, it's okay to let others acknowledge your leadership, but be sure you include and acknowledge your team as well. For instance, if there is a special edition of the organizational newsletter to share the vision with employees, a team picture might be more appropriate than one of your magnificent mug shots. If you go on the road to share and discuss the vision with employee groups, take along a couple of team members and let them conduct the meetings. In short, share the limelight.

To you as a Performer, the envisioning initiative is complete after the vision is communicated. However, in reality it's just beginning. Holding yourself and others accountable and tracking ongoing progress are critical. You must design, implement, and manage the process that translates the vision into discrete activities and ultimately into operations planning and budgeting. For instance, bimonthly or quarterly operations reviews could track progress toward the vision targets as well as near-term financial results and annual goals. If you don't track progress with regard to the vision, or you delegate the tracking of progress (which you might have a tendency to do), you will send the wrong message and negate some of the impact and importance of the vision. The vision would then become merely words.

To support the creation of a bold vision, it will be necessary for you as a leader to carry out leadership initiative #2: managing personal, individual, and team mindsets. Working in tandem, envisioning and managing mindsets create the foundation for the remaining eight leadership initiatives.

INITIATIVE 2: MANAGING MINDSETS

Removing "Blinders" to Problems, Opportunities, and New Possibilities

Complements Envisioning

Getting yourself and others to create a vision is only half the battle. Once the envisioning process is under way, you will become aware of the different ways you and others see your enterprise. These differing mindsets, or frames of reference, make it difficult to create a *really* new organizational future. Initial attempts to create a vision typically yield only a variation of what is already possible and probable. A good example comes from a struggling aerospace company whose old vision was "to be the supplier of choice" for customers worldwide. In discussions with the newly appointed CEO, I asked, "Aren't you *already* the supplier of choice?" "Pretty much," he said. "We need a new future, but we can't get out of the box."

The "box" my client was referring to was the collective mindset of his organization—hidden assumptions about the business they were in. By limiting mindsets, leaders were focusing this aerospace company on a market that was experiencing intense international competition. For this organization's leaders to move the organization beyond their static vision statement, managing mindsets would be a necessary part of their new envisioning process.

Like the other leadership initiatives, managing mindsets defines leadership and differentiates it from management. Managers make the best use of resources. Leaders make new resources possible by increasing what is possible for an organization to achieve.

PURPOSE of Managing Mindsets

As a leader of an organization you have individual mindsets, and your corporation or agency has shared beliefs that define and limit your performance. For example, how successful you'll be in a new job depends as much on how knowledgeable and competent you *think* you are, as on how knowledgeable and competent you *really* are. If you feel competent, you will act that way. You will inspire confidence, make forceful decisions, take prudent risks and, in general, become and be perceived as competent.

Your organization has a shared or collective mindset called *dominant logic* that unites it, but also blinds it to both problems and possibilities. A classic example of dominant logic was IBM's belief in the '60s and '70s that mainframe and minicomputers were the way of the future. IBM executives were certainly aware of the burgeoning microcomputer industry, but "IBM was in the mainframe and minicomputer business." That mindset or dominant logic blinded them and put IBM in the hole they're still digging out of today.

Identifying and then scrutinizing your organization's dominant logic has strategic benefits beyond the creation of a vision. Managing or expanding organizational mindsets allows you to see competitors as potential partners, vendors as planners, and customers as design engineers. In short, this second leadership initiative not only leads to new processes and products, but to new resources, as well.

Mindsets are insidious because we frequently are not aware of them. As members of an organization, we operate much like a bird in a cage. To the bird the world is about two cubic feet in size and that's all there is. We know the bird is in an artificial enclosure, but only because we're not in the cage. We all operate in a "cage" of sorts and businesses do, too. Managing mindsets involves a process of helping ourselves and the people in our organization see the artificial boundaries that limit our vision of the future. This initiative opens the door to our organizational cage.

INDICATORS That Managing Mindsets Is Needed

Mindsets are difficult to manage because they are difficult for you to see. Like the bird in the cage, you are trapped by limiting beliefs about your customers, products, capabilities, and so on. And, while it is difficult to see these assumptions, there are telltale signs, indicators that mindsets may be limiting your business opportunities. The following indicators should register a *mental alarm* that limiting mindset barriers may be present within your organization. If you put a check in two or more of the boxes below, you and your team may be operating at a disadvantage due to limiting mindsets.

- ❏ A new vision statement looks like the old one or everyone likes the old vision just fine.

- ❏ Business growth, as measured in total sales or the ratio of revenue per customer, is less than five percent a year.

- ❏ Lack of new blood—no new members have been added to your leadership team within the past two years.

❑ Your current and future strategy is primarily one of cost reduction—you're competing on the basis of cost alone.

❑ Your leadership team is split into two or more distinct (and often warring) factions with regard to your company's future direction.

The last indicator—significant differences of opinion about what future direction should be taken—occurs because organization mindsets disintegrate person by person, not all at once. As they do, differences of opinion, and often conflicts, develop because members of your team no longer hold the same mindsets. To one group of people on your team, your company's future depends on the ongoing success of one of your core products or services. To another group, further investment in that core product or service is useless because the future lies in an entirely new product. Who's right? Maybe neither. The best way to find out is to initiate the managing mindsets process.

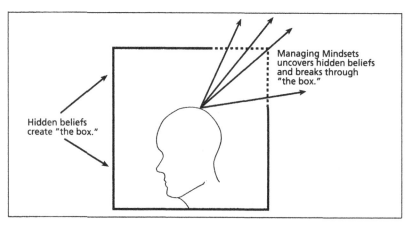

Managing Mindsets uncovers hidden beliefs and breaks through "the box."

Hidden beliefs create "the box."

Managing Mindsets Model

The Managing Mindsets PROCESS

When I initially asked John (the CEO of an aerospace company) what business he was in, he gave a reflex answer—"We build airplanes." The fact that his answer came too quickly told me John may be operating under an unexamined assumption. Only when I probed, essentially asking that same question over and over, did John realize he was answering automatically, with little thought. The moment he reflected on that "We build airplanes" mindset, it lost its hold on his mind. John became able to envision that he was really in the environmental systems business.

Even if John had decided to remain exclusively in the aerospace industry, it would have been a *considered choice,* not a reflex response based upon a hidden mindset. Essentially, that's what the managing mindsets process does—makes limiting mindsets disappear by simply making you and others aware of them.

You might be surprised by your team's assumptions about your products, services, customers, market segment, niche, public perceptions, employee attitudes, financial condition, or even the core business you're in. As an introduction to the envisioning process, assemble those responsible for developing the vision and initiate the following three-step process:

1. Reveal the assumptions you and your team hold with regard to an issue or decision. Record these assumptions on a flip chart or whiteboard.

2. Review this list of organizational assumptions, asking individuals to indicate whether he or she personally believes each of the assumptions. This can be done by raising hands, balloting, etc.

3. Share and discuss the results of this inquiry.

This process will yield commonly held assumptions that delineate the boundaries of the "box" people in your organization operate within. Getting the collective mindsets out in the open allows you to determine if your box is smaller than it needs to be. Unfortunately, we will always be holding some limiting beliefs and thus will be operating within a box of sorts. However, the bigger our box is, the greater the potential business opportunities. For example, do you sell bakeware to U.S. homemakers or sheet metal products to the world? The same knowledge, skills, and much of the same equipment are used in both.

A recent example of mindset breakthroughs occurred with a friend of mine who owns and operates an exotic jewelry store. She used to get most of her products from Bali, Indonesia. However, a business breakthrough occurred during one of our conversations when she was talking about the fun she had on buying trips. My friend realized that her mindset was to *bring jewelry to the customers*. Now she *takes customers to the jewelry,* organizing and managing buying trips to Bali for jewelry and gift store owners.

The strategic shift from taking jewelry to customers to taking customers to the jewelry seemed to happen with little or no external facilitation. My friend was able to burst out of the box herself, with little or no help from me. She had a natural ability to manage mindsets. Your ability to manage mindsets depends, to a large degree, on your leadership style, as the next section points out.

Your NATURAL ABILITY for Managing Mindsets

Your ability to manage mindsets is determined by your innate openness to new ideas and your willingness to be introspective. These two traits exist, to varying degrees, in each of the four leadership styles. Regardless of your natural ability to manage mindsets, almost every leader can benefit from a facilitator or coach. A facilitator is helpful when dismantling limiting mindsets, because he or she doesn't share them with you. An outside facilitator stands outside your box. If you bristle at the notion of facilitator, know that your discomfort may be a reflection of your leadership style.

◆ Managing Mindsets for the COMMANDER

Natural Ability Index: 3

As a Commander, you tend to take a direct route when addressing an issue and have a capacity for honest self-examination. While these tendencies can serve you well in managing mindsets, they are often offset by your need to be right. Even if you become aware of a limiting mindset, you may be reluctant to share it with others. However, self-disclosure is the best way to get others to open up. A simple statement like, "I'm probably harboring some limiting beliefs about our business, customers, products, and services" is all it would take to fully engage your team in the managing mindsets process.

Once the three-step process is under way, try not to evaluate comments and suggestions from others. Your tendency as a Commander to judge others, if expressed, will shut down the discussion and the process. Be aware of your facial expressions and body language, too. Watch what magically happens when you create a nonjudgmental discussion.

You're not crazy about facilitators and that's all right. You don't need one if you monitor your own verbal and nonverbal tendency to judge what others say. Just be aware that others are watching for your not-too-well-hidden reactions.

♣ Managing Mindsets for the STRATEGIST

Natural Ability Index: 10

Any analytical process can be both exhilarating and ex-cruciating for you, the Strategist. For instance, you undoubtedly put more time and effort in annual performance appraisals than anyone else. This tendency to turn ideas and decisions over and over, can work *for you* when managing mindsets. You are methodical and thoughtful, particularly when it comes to big, strategic decisions. Where others on your management team might automatically assume that what has made your company successful in the past will make it successful in the future, you won't be as quick to agree. Share your hesitation and your awareness of your own limiting assumptions. Your willingness to be fair makes you particularly adept at this leadership initiative.

A good approach for you is to introduce the concept to the team and then ask all the members to reflect on the mindsets that might be present. Have them make a list, which they can then bring back to discuss as a group. You might also invite team members to meet with you privately to discuss an issue. When it comes time for a large group discussion, you might benefit from a facilitator who will help you manage your tendency to be dogmatic. One of the richest catalysts for your leadership development involves confronting and managing the belief that *your* way is always best.

♥ Managing Mindsets for the COACH

Natural Ability Index: 7

As a Coach, your only real difficulty with managing mindsets is coming to grips with your inherent distaste for conflict in any form. Managing mindsets can be an emotional and sometimes volatile process. When conflicts emerge, don't back off. Remember the object is not to argue points of view, but simply to let them surface, and then examine them. Allow your natural tendency to limit open conflict; remind teammates that there's no right or wrong assumption. Help them see things through your eyes. While you have a natural facilitating ability, if you expect significant conflicting assumptions among team members, bring in an outside person to assist in this process.

♠ Managing Mindsets for the PERFORMER

Natural Ability Index: 5

If you are a Performer, your open-mindedness and creativity serve you well. For instance, with your guidance, a simple off-site management meeting can quickly become an exciting event by including outside speakers, facilitated breakout sessions, recreation, and entertainment. In short, you usually transcend the paradigm for whatever you take on. You can leverage this tendency to push at traditional boundaries when it comes to managing mindsets. You'll no doubt lead the way into the exploration of hidden assumptions with your team, and you'll make it an exciting experience in the bargain.

You have influence over many members of your management team and are very persuasive. However, this gift is also what makes managing mindsets somewhat difficult for you. You must discuss where you personally stand without trying to influence others. A facilitator could help you manage your tendency to dominate the discussion and *sell* others your viewpoint.

These two acts—envisioning and managing mindsets—will enable you and your management team to determine the proper strategic direction for your enterprise. Managing mindsets is a process that helps people realize that the organization's future need not be a slightly different version of its past. Your company has the skill sets, the customer base, and the financial resources to go into new, previously unthought-of, directions. With a clear direction in mind, you are ready to rally your employees, shareholders, customers, and other stakeholders. That's the objective of the next initiative—modeling.

INITIATIVE 3: MODELING

Creating Linkage with Key Stakeholders

If there is one leadership act everyone knows intuitively, it's modeling. Indeed, whenever I ask someone what a leader does, modeling always tops the list. Although different terms are used to describe this initiative, nearly everyone agrees that a leader should personally and regularly meet with employees, customers, shareholders, community leaders, and the media. Some people call this public relations; but the modeling initiative involves more than that. Modeling requires that you represent *what will be,* as well as what already *is*. This isn't easy. You will find yourself in the tenuous position of modeling existing traditions and values, while at the same time, emulating any new or desired ones.

Modeling is the process that connects and includes all stakeholders with an eye to addressing most of their needs. Every enterprise requires a variety of resources: employees bring knowledge and skills; stockholders invest capital; the media help to create a positive image; and, of course, customers buy products and services and pay the bills. Leaders have to keep each of these groups happy to garner and retain the resources a business needs to grow and prosper. Like many of the other leadership initiatives, modeling is focused on the future. Indeed, you might think of leaders as the custodians of the future.

PURPOSE of Modeling

Modeling systematically connects you with all your stakeholders in a way that allows you to hear, understand and, as much as possible, meet their needs. However, since it's nearly impossible to meet all their numerous, and oftentimes conflicting needs, you must also make a commitment that most of their needs will *eventually* be met. This acknowledgment allows them to compromise some short-term needs and continue to commit themselves and their resources to your enterprise. The concept behind modeling is simple: to keep your stakeholders involved in your company today, they must believe that your enterprise will be as good or better tomorrow. That task of ensuring that improvement will take place falls on your shoulders as a leader.

Modeling requires that you keep a tenuous balance among the needs of *all* stakeholders so that no one group gets its needs met at the expense of the others. Through a well-planned and managed series of news conferences, meetings, presentations, TV appearances, and social events, you forge relationships and open communication channels to employees, customers, the media, union officials, government agencies, and stockholders. For example, if the stockholders' need for higher dividends is ignored, your company may be deprived of capital needed for research, improvements, and expansion.

While it may seem nearly impossible to pay too much attention to customers, it can happen. One of my clients spent thousands of dollars on a new computer system to track the status of custom-built windows and doors during the manufacturing process, because a customer focus group indicated customers wanted status reports on large orders. As it turned out, the system was rarely used and created unnecessary overhead. Customers can sometimes ask for what they *think they want,* rather than what they truly *need.* In the end, these window and door customers only needed assurance they would get their orders on time, not daily manufacturing status reports.

Several departments in your company or organization interface with the customer. The public relations department deals with the media and public; other groups deal with shareholders and so forth. However, as the leader you are the only person with the ability and responsibility to interface with *all* of them. To do so, you need a broad knowledge base from which to conduct briefings, meetings, and negotiations, make requests, and collect feedback from diverse stakeholder groups. Modeling is one of the most demanding leadership initiatives. The schedule alone can run you ragged.

No one knows that better than Harvard University president, Dr. Neil Rudenstine. Running a major university today means mediating among faculty members, students, alumni, administrators, donors, trustees, and the public. After three years of putting the modeling initiative into action at meetings, ceremonies, cocktail parties, presentations, and speeches, Dr. Rudenstine was forced to take a temporary leave, suffering from sheer exhaustion. However, most organizations suffer from too little modeling, rather than too much. The list of indicators will give you a way to know if that's true of your company.

INDICATORS That Modeling Is Needed

When the modeling initiative is totally lacking, an organization is usually experiencing several problems. If the need for modeling is not heeded, you may find yourself dealing with such traumatic events as:

- A strike—if you don't connect with employees;
- Rapidly declining sales—if you don't listen to customers;
- Damaging news stories—if you ignore media inquiries; or
- A rapid decline in the price of your stock—if you don't heed Wall Street analysts or shareholder communications.

However, there are also less dramatic indicators that modeling is needed. Certain behaviors, circumstances, and events will tell you if modeling is being called for. After taking an inventory of how you think you handle the modeling initiative, review the indicators list that follows. If you check two or more of the boxes below, modeling may be needed.

❑ You consistently send other people to represent your company to interact, negotiate, or communicate with your stakeholders (either the same individual or a different representative to each constituency).

❑ You notice a conscious and consistent effort on the part of team members to suggest that *others* rather than you represent the enterprise.

❑ You notice that there is a wide gap in perception and opinion among your stakeholder groups (i.e., the customers love you, but your employees mistrust you).

❑ Your vision and strategy are focused almost entirely on one stakeholder (e.g., stockholders).

❑ One or more of your key stakeholders unite in overt opposition to your organization's leadership (e.g., an employee strike, a customer boycott, or a shareholder resolution).

Of course, you don't need *external* indicators to know that modeling is needed. One of the best indicators that modeling is called for can be found *inside* you. How do you feel about your role as a model or representative? Do you enjoy it or avoid it? Are you uncomfortable being with some of your stakeholders? How much time do you spend outside your office? Most of the answers to your concerns about leadership are locked inside you.

The Modeling PROCESS

You don't need charisma to be effective at modeling. However, you do need a thorough knowledge of your organization's issues, products, marketplace, financial position, and future direction. That's the ante to get into the leadership game. Furthermore, information you present about your company's plans and direction must be clear, future-oriented, compelling, and consistent. You must present the *same* key messages whether you are meeting with your management team, presiding over a shareholders' meeting, negotiating with union representatives, interviewing a TV reporter, or cutting the ribbon at a grand opening.

When it comes to modeling, you already carry within yourself all the tools you need. Besides the knowledge and information in your head, you need your mouth to speak, your ears to listen, and your gut for intuition. As a leader you must not only hear what people say, but understand their emotions, frustrations, concerns, and commitments. That's where your gut comes in. If you listen with your whole self, you'll make a solid connection with your stakeholders. **The greatest need all stakeholders have is to be heard at the deepest level.** That is why modeling must be done in person.

While you can easily acquire knowledge and develop listening skills, the ability to model is heavily dependent on your leadership style and *flexibility*. While style flexibility is required for all types of leaders, if you're a Strategist or Coach, you'll especially need to hone your *style-shifting* skills.

Style shifting involves intentionally matching the style of the person or persons you're interacting with so that you can establish rapport. (This process will be discussed in a later chapter.) Be aware that modeling requires you to operate in all leadership styles. One circumstance may call for the calm diplomatic response of the Strategist. The next may require the firm stand of the Commander. The one after that may need a compromising negotiation led by the Coach. Yet another circumstance may call for the quick wit of the Performer to get out of a tight spot. Most individuals are not born with that kind of style flexibility. It must be learned and practiced.

Your NATURAL ABILITY for Modeling

Modeling is one initiative dramatically affected by leadership style. Modeling fits the stereotypical idea of a leader as a highly visible, charismatic person. To a large degree, strong interpersonal skills can make you naturally adept at modeling. However, it is possible to use your own, albeit less gregarious, style and still accomplish all the objectives of modeling. The following coaching tips will help you leverage your strengths and manage your weaknesses.

◆ Modeling for the COMMANDER

Natural Ability Index: 9

Your "take charge" attitude, high energy, and straightforward manner make you adept at modeling. Your natural future-orientation and no-nonsense approach have appeal for stockholders, customers, and media alike. If you're having difficulties, it's not your way to hedge, so admit it and get right into how you intend to address these problems. Sometimes, your non-emotional manner can lead employees to feel that you are not empathetic or caring. The key to improving rapport with this group lies in learning to listen.

As a Commander, you have good negotiating ability, because your honest nature and willingness to argue a point without recrimination win you the respect that is critical in any negotiation. Sometimes, however, your need to be in control can make negotiations frustrating for you. Keep a lid on your temper and hang in there.

While you likely feel comfortable with nearly any of your constituencies, they may not feel the same way about you. Your tendency to dominate, combined with your sometimes hurried and abrupt manner, can put people off, particularly team members and employees. Although it may not be your preferred way to operate, it would be helpful to bring along one or more teammates to meetings, negotiations, and even presentations. Teaming up with individuals with more people-oriented leadership styles, like a Performer or Coach, balances your task orientation.

♣ Modeling for the STRATEGIST

Natural Ability Index: 1

When you think about modeling, that knot in your gut is telling you this is not one of your favorite initiatives, but you are better prepared than you may think. You have the facts and the ability to analyze and understand data and information better than most. Indeed, when you are sure of your information, you present it in a powerful, clear, well-organized, and persuasive manner. Even so, you may find yourself limiting or even avoiding more public engagements, a tendency that may have to do with a misperception about modeling.

Keep in mind that modeling is not just smiling, shaking hands, making speeches and, in general, "looking good." To be successful at modeling, you must have a firm grasp of your present business circumstances and have set a clear, concise, and positive future direction. Preparation is the key.

Meetings with community groups, customers, or the media may cause concern because of unexpected questions and the expectation of immediate answers. If you're put off by answering some legitimate questions, it may be misunderstood as indecision or, worse yet, being uninformed. One of the best ways to prepare for an open-ended question and answer session is to ask your staff to prepare a complete list of possible questions, along with well-researched answers. Being prepared for the unexpected will give you the confidence you need to be successful in any modeling situation. One final tip—smile!

Modeling for the COACH

Natural Ability Index: 3

As a Coach, you have many qualities that can make modeling one of your strong suits. Your warm and friendly manner and excellent listening ability make you likable. Although you may be less outgoing than you would wish, you are fine as long as you don't try to be someone you're not.

Being a peacemaker at heart, you would be invaluable in resolving conflict and stalled negotiations, so look for those opportunities. However, in negotiations you may have a tendency to give away too much, particularly if you think resistance will cause problems. Indeed, your people orientation can leave you wide open to unreasonable employee demands. Your best approach in negotiations, or when confronted with employee demands, is to get clear on those areas and points that are negotiable, and those that are not, *before* you begin. If you are called upon to reconsider your position, you'll be better off doing so in a separate, more private meeting in which you get the advice of others. The most difficult part of modeling for you is the inevitable negative feedback you will get. You can be overly sensitive to criticism. Prepare yourself psychologically to be rejected. Your stakeholder constituency is so diverse that it is impossible to please everyone all the time. When preparing and gathering feedback from others, make sure you and your staff give as much weight to the positive feedback as you do to the negative. Keeping these ideas in mind will help you change a weakness in this area into a strength.

♠ Modeling for the PERFORMER

Natural Ability Index: 10

Modeling comes naturally to you as a Performer. Your energy, enthusiasm, and normally excellent speaking ability make you an effective spokesperson with almost every stakeholder group. If anything, you might rely on your charisma too much. You should probably spend a little more time preparing: getting background information and learning all the issues. To you the preparation may seem boring, but it's necessary (and it will make you effective).

When with others, guard against your tendency to dominate the conversation and be the center of attention. Many modeling situations call for you to share the stage and acknowledge others. If you're not careful, you can be a hit with the fans, but strike out with the people with whom you work. Bring along a trusted associate, whose coaching may keep you from stealing the limelight or making rash commitments. Your impulsive nature can lead to quick answers and unconsidered promises. Involving a colleague could help give you additional time and counsel. When you finally do make a commitment, be sure to follow through. You are a leader, and people take even your most casual promises seriously.

At the heart of modeling is the notion that a leader is a symbol of the enterprise. A leader embodies the basic characteristics and qualities of an organization, particularly its values. For that reason, clarifying personal and organizational values is the next complementary initiative.

INITIATIVE 4: CLARIFYING VALUES

Leveraging the Primary Drivers of Organizational Behavior

Complements Modeling

Values provide the foundation upon which your company's future is built. Values drive actions, both individually and collectively. For example, most of the policies and laws in the United States are built upon a belief in individual freedom and respect for all people. These collective values direct and shape our behavior individually (e.g., charitable contributions) and collectively as a nation (e.g., foreign policy). Most people would agree it is our values that have made our country successful. Using arithmetic logic: if values drive actions, and actions drive results and success, then values drive success.

VALUES ➤ ACTION ➤ RESULTS ➤ SUCCESS

The fourth leadership initiative of clarifying values complements modeling because shared values are the "glue" that holds an organization's stakeholders together. Without a common set of values, the behavior of employees, shareholders, opinion leaders, and other stakeholders may become arbitrary and self-serving. However, as a leader if you communicate and share common values, you can maintain a strong relationship with your stakeholders, even if you don't meet all their immediate needs. For instance, employees may be frightened by the prospect of a merger, but if your company has demonstrated that it values loyalty and fairness, employees will be supportive during the merger effort, knowing they will be treated fairly.

As part of the modeling process, in meetings, negotiations, presentations, press conferences, and the like, you will want to communicate and act in a manner consistent with your company's values. For starters, that means your leadership team must align on a common set of values. The time invested in clarifying values pays big dividends because a common set of values not only influences stakeholder relationships, but every aspect of your business.

PURPOSE of Clarifying Values

In addition to shaping the key messages communicated during the modeling initiative, identifying your organization's core values serves another important purpose. It makes your organization *credible* and ultimately *viable*. As such, values have more to do with the *long-term* success of your enterprise than does your strategic plan, which traditionally gets much more attention.

Values are threads that tie your mission, vision, and strategic planning together. If your mission, vision, and strategy are inconsistent with your stated or implicit values, your organization will lack credibility with employees. As a result, they will not wholeheartedly implement your vision or strategy because values are the *primary* drivers of human behavior. For instance, there are laws against stealing. But the law is not what stops most people from stealing; rather it's their personal, family, and community values.

In organizations the mission, vision, and strategy tell employees where they should be focusing their attention, energy, and resources. But if your mission, vision, and strategic plan are in any way inconsistent with your organization's values, these planning tools lose their power. Without agreement on a common set of values, your organization will be like a leaf blowing in the wind, tossed around by the whims of a strong stakeholder group, the current fads of the marketplace, and sometimes the unethical behavior of employees. The net effect is a waste of time, money, and human energy.

The process for clarifying values not only seeks to identify and rank your organization's core values, but examines your mission, vision, strategy, policies, and structure to see if they are consistent with those values. If not, it's unlikely your strategy will be properly executed or your vision realized. Values guide decision-making and all organizational behavior. Clarifying values enables you to align and focus human energy to maximize scarce resources and unite your stakeholders. That's *not* "soft stuff," as some of my clients are apt to say when I first introduce the clarifying values initiative. **Values have as much impact on an organization's success as a good strategic plan**.

INDICATORS that Clarifying Values Is Needed

One company leader whom I coached, Bruce, was struggling to reconcile what seemed to be a paradox. On the one hand, his employees said they didn't know in what direction the company was going; on the other, he knew the vision and strategic plan had been communicated because he did it personally in a series of meetings. It wasn't a paradox at all. Our coaching session revealed two indicators clarifying values was needed.

The fact that Bruce wanted to revisit his original vision, together with pervasive employee complaints about the lack of direction, tipped me off. The actions he was taking were not consistent with the long-standing values of his company. It wasn't so much that the direction Bruce and the management team had set was unclear, but rather that the way they were going about changing direction was inconsistent with existing values. What follows is a list of indicators that should alert you to the need to clarify values:

❑ Pervasive complaints with regard to knowing the "direction" an organization is going—oftentimes despite extensive communications;

❑ Calls from the board of directors or shareholders for new leadership;

❑ Changes in vision and strategy that are triggered by changes in leadership rather than changes in the industry and marketplace;

❑ Growing awareness of inconsistent and/or conflicting policies and practices (often manifested in increasing staff and budget in the employee relations function).

On a more extreme note . . .

❑ Unethical and/or illegal behavior within an organization;

❑ An increasing number of lawsuits by employees.

In addition, there are certain business activities which, in and of themselves, should trigger the clarifying values initiative. They include:

❑ The onset of any negotiations with regard to a merger, acquisition, or strategic alliance.

❑ The initiation of a mission and/or vision creation process.

❑ Major changes on the leadership team, particularly if the team leader and/or other members come from outside the organization.

There are also more subtle *internal* indicators that clarifying values is needed—for instance, a dissonance created when you no longer know what's important to your company. Your values must be consistent with those of the organization; if not, your actions will be inconsistent. A clash of personal values and organizational values creates enormous stress, contributes to low morale, and generates a host of dysfunctional behaviors among stakeholders. Getting in touch with your personal values is an important part of the clarifying values process.

The Clarifying Values PROCESS

Clarifying values is the work of leaders and leadership *teams*, those who manage the majority of your organization's capital and human resources. If your organization is only 20 people, the clarifying values process might well include everyone. In larger organizations, this process can be conducted by the executive team—typically the top 8 to 12 managers.

The values clarification process can be carried out within a meeting, a workshop, or even in a planned series of dialogues. The objective is to identify and define three or four core values that every employee knows and to which the leadership holds their actions accountable. As it is with the development of a vision and mission, it is during the discussion that the values derive their meaning. For example, a value like "maximizing individual potential" can mean many things to many people. It is the inquiry, dialogue, and debate among members of the leadership team that give this value the depth of meaning necessary to make it actionable. It is in the course of discussing this value that the team determines that "maximizing individual potential" means giving employees equal access to new positions and training classes, or allowing time off for employees receiving non-work-related education. There are two kinds of values: foundational and operational. Maximizing individual potential is an example of a foundational value. Foundational values are intrinsic traits that form the basic character of an organization. There are also operational values. Operational values provide direction and suggest a specific action. Ideally, an organization should have a blend of both. The following statements were pulled from transcripts of keynote addresses from three company presidents. They clearly state company values in a way that employees, customers, shareholders, and all stakeholders can understand.

From an automotive company:

Foundational Value: "Become the standard by which others are judged."

Operational Value: "The customer is the focus of everything we do."

From a computer manufacturing company:

Foundational Value: "People, workers, management, and company are all the same."

Operational Value: "Every employee must benefit from the company's success."

From a computer software company:

Foundational Value: "We believe in security . . . the permanence and development of people."

Operational Value: "We use first names and believe in open communication."

Once your organization's team has reached an awareness and appreciation of the need for clarifying values that must be foundational and operational, you must design a meeting process in which you and your team accomplish the following five steps:

1. Explore your personal values.
2. Identify, define, and align on organizational values.
3. Rank organizational values—foundational and operational combined—and emphasize the top three or four core values.
4. Take definitive action to ensure that the core values are reflected in the organization's mission, vision, and strategy and are systematically integrated into the policies, systems, practices, and procedures of your organization.
5. Continuously communicate and model the core values.

To offer a bit of coaching, there is a natural tendency to want to communicate your team's values after the first three steps in the process. This is a mistake. Put your values to work in your policies, vision, and strategy. Communicating a list of values before they are actually reflected in tangible ways can turn a values statement into hollow words.

Your NATURAL ABILITY for Clarifying Values

The creation of your personal values is a complex process that involves the environment you grew up in, your family experiences, role models, and your personal experiences. Your leadership style also influences your personal values, as well as how you *manifest* those values. In addition, your leadership style will dictate how you approach the clarifying values process, as you put this initiative to work in your organization.

◆ Clarifying Values for the COMMANDER

Natural Ability Index: 4

Throughout much of your life you have likely found yourself in leadership roles, which have given you an *intuitive* appreciation of values. However, as an organizational leader, you may have a tendency to undervalue the human side of the business and be tempted to put your energies elsewhere. This would be a mistake. One of the biggest areas of your leadership development lies in expanding your ability to balance the technical and human sides of the business.

When you *clarify values,* one of the biggest stumbling blocks may be sharing your own personal values with others. When the team is identifying and ranking personal and organizational values, a process which often includes a time for private reflection, you may feel more comfortable first writing down your list privately and then discussing your values with the group.

As the five-step clarifying values process unfolds, notice that as a Commander you'll be drawn toward the more action-oriented operational values. That's okay. Just keep in mind that you need the balance that other team members can supply by focusing on foundational values.

♣ Clarifying Values for the STRATEGIST

Natural Ability Index: 8

As a Strategist you may be among the first in your organization to understand the need for the clarifying values initiative, so don't be concerned if others question its need when you suggest it. Guard against your tendency to hold fast to old, existing values. Your organization's foundational values may not change much, if at all, but operational values may need to.

Concerning the five-step process itself, you may be most comfortable giving colleagues time to think things through before discussing organizational values as a group. In this regard, you and the Commander types have something in common. You both may prefer to do a written personal values inventory. However, unlike the Commander, you might want to use a facilitator to aid you and your team with the clarifying values process.

♥ Clarifying Values for the COACH

Natural Ability Index: 9

Clarifying values is just your cup of tea. You intuitively understand and appreciate the importance of clarifying values; you are aware of your own values and are willing to discuss them with others. You'll likely feel more comfortable discussing values, and engaging in a formal process to clarify values, than many of your colleagues. How are you going to deal with their reservations? (Hint: read the coaching tips for the other leadership styles in this section.)

Like the Performer, you as a Coach have a tendency to gravitate toward the foundational values because these tend to be people-oriented and relate to concepts like security, cooperation, and sharing of benefits. Listen to others in the process, who will be advocating more task-oriented, operational values. Ideally you want a balance in your final product—a couple of operational values and a couple of foundational ones.

If you have a weakness with regard to clarifying values, it would be your reluctance to deal with individuals whose values conflict with the rest of the team or organization; because dealing with conflict, in any form, is not your forte. You must remember to put the well-being of the team and organization first, and deal with individuals who are not aligned with the organizational values in private discussions.

♠ Clarifying Values for the PERFORMER

Natural Ability Index: 3

Clarifying values is one of the weaker initiatives for you; not so much because you don't appreciate its importance, but rather that you feel *your* set of values should predominate. You are most interested in those values that speak to creativity and innovation. Such priorities have a rightful place among the organization's values, so hang in there with them. Undoubtedly, having fun is also one of your values and it would be great if you could at least bring up the subject, even if you can't get alignment on "fun" as an official company value. Just be sure to give equal time to more operational values that center around such things as the highest quality products and fair returns for shareholders.

When meeting with your management team to clarify values, you may be inclined to embark on a clarifying values process that "mixes it up," and has a lot of unstructured discussion. If the meeting takes that course, guard against dominating the discussions. Be yourself, but make sure other, less outgoing colleagues have their say as well. If you find this tendency difficult to manage, bring in a skilled facilitator. Your natural compassion and interpersonal communication skill will serve you well regardless of the process used.

Finally, if you have difficulty with any part of the process, it might be following through to ensure that the values are reflected in organizational policies, systems, and practices. It is somewhat tedious work that has little appeal for you. However, it is important work. Policies and procedures reinforce and maintain the desired organizational behaviors, which are driven by values.

INITIATIVE 5: ALIGNING

Unifying People Behind a Decision or Direction

You may be familiar with the general concept of alignment, but may not see it as a distinct leadership act. Aligning is a group decision-making process that *quickly* unites the managers in your organization behind a decision.

One of the most common complaints you'll hear from leaders today is that people may initially agree as a team to take unified action, but later don't support it, and sometimes undermine it. Aligning is a tool that greatly improves the odds that managers in your organization will wholeheartedly follow through on team decisions of which they were a part. This follow-through is critical to the ongoing success of your enterprise and as such, falls into the domain of leadership. In addition, aligning accelerates the decision-making process.

PURPOSE of Aligning

The purpose of aligning is to unify a group of people quickly behind a decision and ensure that they are wholeheartedly engaged in putting that decision into play. When a group decision is made, alignment is usually assumed, but not always achieved, because some elements are often missing from the process. There seems to be a tendency for people to use either-or thinking when making decisions. They believe that a group either reaches a consensus or compromises. Aligning, however, provides a third alternative.

Consensus is difficult to achieve. It is often fraught with conflict and it is time-consuming. As a result, many organizations abandon efforts to reach a consensus, leaving the leader to make unilateral decisions. Although expeditious, one-sided decisions potentially create a rift between the leaders and their teammates, and make it difficult to pass on accountability and responsibility for implementing the decision. In general, people won't take responsibility for decisions they were not a part of. They may comply, but only halfheartedly.

However, there are some pivotal decisions that require consensus, and in these cases it is best to struggle for consensus, no matter how long it takes; for example, involving mergers, strategic alliances, and restructuring. Likewise there are some decisions that should be made by one individual. However, the majority of business decisions fall in between these two extremes, such as merging two functions or operations, making a moderate-sized capital investment, or adding a new product line. The aligning process would assist in making such decisions.

Alignment has most of the advantages of consensus, with few of the downsides of compromise. Aligning avoids weak, fragmented team action and the disintegration of team relationships often associated with other decision-making processes. Aligning can be accomplished quickly, typically in one 60 to 90-minute meeting using a simple six-step process that ensures that every member of the decision-making group is heard. It allows for exploration of options, improves team relationships, and includes everyone in a way that makes united action likely once a final decision has been made. Aligning is a decision-making tool that helps create a *learning organization*—one that explores what works, what doesn't, and why. Too many times, when a decision leads to problems, new solutions are pursued before understanding what was wrong with the old decision. The alignment initiative not only acknowledges that some decisions will require adjustments along the way, but makes it possible to learn from past mistakes. More importantly, alignment improves the quality and speed of decisions overall. Indeed, the key benefit of alignment is decisive execution and follow-through. A decision without follow-through is worse than no decision at all. It wastes valuable time and delivers poor results.

INDICATORS That Aligning Is Needed

Alignment may be new to you and your organization. If so, there may be many indicators that this particular initiative is needed. Look over the checklist below. If the following conditions seem to describe your organization, then aligning may be called for.

❑ Weak or no follow-through by department heads and other managers after they've made a decision.

❑ Implementation programs fraught with problems and conflict, in general, poorly executed decisions.

❑ Finding yourself as a leader making unilateral decisions because the team you're working with can't or won't make timely decisions.

❑ Increasing disintegration of relationships among leadership team members as a consequence of previous decisions. This can show up as bickering during meetings or lack of interaction in the workplace.

❑ Extraordinarily long time frames for making decisions. If you have all the information needed, most business decisions should be made in one meeting.

❑ Long delays in implementation once a decision is made.

❑ A high percentage of decision reversals.

If several of the above indicators are present, it's time to introduce aligning to your team and give it a try.

The Alignment PROCESS

Since aligning is a *team* decision-making process, it works best when relationships between team members are already strong. If not, additional team-building efforts and/or individual coaching can be deployed to "clean up" past transgressions, build a new foundation for interpersonal communication, and leave the team committed to working together. There are many ways to accomplish this. For example, a workshop on leadership style and how it affects behavior and relationships can help build a solid foundation for teamwork. As you will discover, the alignment process itself has an added team-building benefit because it is built on the belief that every person's contribution, no matter how diverse, is valuable and useful. One of the best ways to introduce the alignment process to your team is by leading a well structured discussion, which can be divided into three parts.

1. Explore the concept of alignment and dispel false assumptions.

In the first part of your team discussion, your objective is to create awareness that, in the long run, *team relationships* are as important as any decision. Your team will make hundreds, if not thousands, of decisions each year. Business success requires a series of good decisions. Therefore, if individuals on your team find themselves at odds with colleagues on any particular issue, it's often better to go along if you can, in order to preserve the goodwill and cooperative spirit you will rely upon in future decisions. During this initial part of the discussion, you can set the right tone by expressing your confidence in the *collective wisdom* of your team. Indeed, that is one of the premises of this decision-making process. The structured process itself dispels parochial thinking and political motives. Once those limiting factors are set aside, your team's collective knowledge and experience can come to the fore.

Aligning is also based upon a simple awareness that group decision-making tends to be lengthy, not because there is *total* disagreement among members of the group, but because many of the members disagree with *part* of the decision. There's an 80/20 rule that applies to decision-making. As a team approaches alignment, the majority of the members can agree with 80% of the decision. They tend to hold out in order to change the 20% they disagree with. This situation is dealt with during the alignment process by leaving the door open to adjustments after implementation begins.

At this early part of the discussion, you must dispel two limiting assumptions. The first is that differences of opinion are bad. Logic and experience tell a different story. Differences are the catalyst for innovation and creative action. The second limiting assumption is that holding an opinion different from that of other team members indicates that an individual cannot act with the team after an opposing decision is made. Having a difference of opinion does not preclude someone from being a team player.

2. Lay out five operating guidelines for the alignment process.

- There must be a sufficient number of choices or possibilities. You can't expect a team to align if there are only one or two options.

- Each member of the group making the decision must be able to speak freely and (most importantly) be heard at a deep level.

- After aligning, there must be an opportunity for team members to share any unexpressed communications and feelings and, if possible, share their commitment to support the aligned decision.

- Team members need to understand that the time required to reach alignment on any one decision will vary with the difficulty of the decision. It can take from as little as 30 minutes to as long as a day. In some cases, the process can include a break for reflection.

3. Initiate the six-step alignment process.

- Ask every individual gathered to make the decision to state clearly and concisely where each stands with regard to an issue or idea. People should only speak once, unless they change their minds as they hear others speak. If someone's statement is not clear, you and others can ask questions. As their leader, you should speak last.

- Next, ask people to share what they heard and what points they feel the team, as a whole, seems to agree on. Everyone need not speak.

- After several team members have shared their ideas, consolidate their interpretations into a brief, carefully worded summary statement, outlining the decision the team seems to be aligning on. As the leader and champion of the alignment process, you need to ensure the wording of the decision that your team seems to be aligning upon is clear and precise.

- Share your summary of the team's decision and ask others to comment on it. It's sometimes helpful to write the summary statement on a whiteboard or flip chart and let team members edit it. At this juncture, you should make the point that there will also be room for adjustments during the implementation process. Do not allow individuals to use this step to make final appeals for their viewpoint.

- After hearing and seeing the feedback, make necessary adjustments to your statement and share the revised statement with the team, asking for more feedback. Keep doing this until there are no additional changes and you hear comments indicating general concurrence. When this happens, you can move on to the final step.

- State the "final" decision clearly. As you do, make the point that it is only prudent to remain open to making adjustments as the decision is implemented. Stress the word "adjustments." It doesn't mean changing the decision itself, but only some aspects of it.

After completing the six steps, systematically ask team members to "say whatever they want or need to say about the final decision." It is important to leave a wide opening for people. You want to hear *anything* they have to say. In most cases, you will get positive comments and promises of support. Even if individuals are not in total agreement, they need the opportunity to say they will support the team and the decision.

These six steps, along with the introductory discussion, will ensure that alignment is taking place. You will soon discover that alignment results in high quality decisions, facilitates unified action, fosters trust, engenders respect, and enhances team relationships.

Your NATURAL ABILITY for Aligning

◆ Aligning for the COMMANDER

Natural Ability Index: 7

Your *"damn the torpedoes, full steam ahead"* attitude makes it more likely that as a Commander you will miss the signs that aligning is needed. You may want to reread the "Indicators" section in this chapter. Your domineering manner tends to create "yes people" who unfortunately just say "Yes" when you're around. This kind of situation could complicate the alignment process and give you the illusion of alignment. Your ability to respect honest differences of opinion can work for you during the alignment process, so use it. Surface different opinions, and don't quash dissent.

Alignment can be a breakthrough in leadership development for you. You like to make decisions and take action, but you sometimes leave other team members behind. While this approach works in the short term and delivers results, it creates relationship problems. Aligning offers you a way out of this dilemma, by speeding up decisive action and bringing everyone along.

Possibly the biggest problem you have with regard to aligning is facilitating the process itself. As a Commander you run meetings like a conductor runs a train. When it's time to roll out, everyone had better be on board. However, now that you have considered the importance of aligning, give the process time. Ultimately, you'll get a decision and unified, decisive action.

♣ Aligning for the STRATEGIST

Natural Ability Index: 4

Decision-making tends to be an agonizing process for you as a Strategist. Your tendency to be a perfectionist can play havoc with your business and your team. Aligning may provide one avenue through which you can make decisions more quickly and get your team in action sooner. In fact, aligning can help you address what traditionally is a troublesome area for you: decision-making. You like the fact that aligning facilitates higher quality decisions, and you appreciate its structured approach. In particular, the exploration of all options has appeal for you. While it involves more people than you might prefer, it does facilitate a thoroughness that you value.

Concerning the step-by-step alignment process, you may be more comfortable with longer sessions where you have time to reflect. This is fine as long as you don't turn aligning into a drawn-out process.

♥ Aligning for the COACH

Natural Ability Index: 6

For you, aligning is an easy concept to understand and appreciate, but a difficult one to master. Your natural ability to facilitate discussions and include everyone makes the aligning initiative appealing to you. However, alignment is different from *consensus,* your preferred method of operation; you may have a tendency to strive for consensus once you get into the alignment process. Just stick with the six-step process, and don't prolong any of the steps in an attempt to get consensus. In short, properly structured and facilitated, aligning can give you a way to deal with difficult people and situations.

The alignment process also offers a means to keep one or two team members from dominating team discussions and decision-making. Your fear of creating conflict sometimes makes you too patient with people who take over at meetings. The highly structured alignment process gives you a useful tool to manage this tendency. Perhaps the main benefit of alignment for you is that you will be less likely to put your own needs last. With alignment, everyone is heard and gets equal time. If, in the course of the alignment process, people become tense, and discussion strained, remember that the overall process *improves* teamwork and team relationships.

♠ Aligning for the PERFORMER

Natural Ability Index: 6

Aligning should be an easy addition to your repertoire as a Performer. Your inherent flexibility and interpersonal approach to decision-making actually make facilitating the alignment process a natural. However, your tendency to *persuade* and dominate discussions can get in the way. Mastering alignment requires discipline and, for you, a degree of self-monitoring. Watch yourself and the time. If you cannot manage your talkative ways, aligning discussions can become too long and others may not be able to fully participate. A facilitator can help in this area.

As you review the six-step alignment process, you may have found yourself discounting its highly structured format. You prefer more freewheeling discussions. Just remember it is the very precise structure of aligning that makes it work, so try to stick with it. There are plenty of other opportunities for you to wax poetic. A common reaction to the aligning initiative is that it's easier said than done. So it is. However, the bridging initiative, which we'll discuss next, complements aligning and takes some of the "wrinkles" out of the process.

INITIATIVE 6: BRIDGING

Moving Individuals into Alignment with the Larger Group

Complements Aligning

Bridging is the creation of an intellectual and emotional link between individuals and a group, using a structured one-on-one conversation. Bridging complements aligning by persuading individuals to support a team decision with which they mostly disagree. The bridging initiative provides a much needed "time out" so individuals can break out of their either-or thinking that says, "Either I must agree wholeheartedly, or disagree."

This initiative can be looked at as a *coaching conversation* in which the individuals being coached no longer resist a decision they did not agree with. Its purpose is to bring individuals "back into the fold" by enabling them to find ways to meet their personal needs *within* the intended actions of the team. Without bridging, some individuals may be left out of the decision-making process. As a consequence, they will not take decisive action to implement a team decision, and in some cases, directly or indirectly resist or undermine the actions of the team. As a leader, one of your primary concerns is holding your team together. Bridging is a helpful tool for unifying a team and maintaining team relationships in the face of disagreements.

PURPOSE of Bridging

In your leadership role, you are refereeing a continual struggle between individual and group needs. While most people say that they want a strong leader who stands for what *he or she* believes, what they really want is a leader who stands for what *they* believe—someone who agrees with them. This tug-of-war generates tension, frustration, and often conflict. Such is the case with the alignment process, where individuals are asked to put the needs of the team before their own. The bridging initiative reconciles this emotional dilemma.

With a structured alignment process, it is much easier to make a *reasonable* choice. However, human emotions are not subject to reasoning alone. The bridging act provides a way to deal constructively with the residual *emotional issues* that often remain after alignment. Bridging "defuses" an "emotional time bomb" that would eventually go off, allowing an aligned decision to be sustained.

The bridging initiative *strengthens* the personal relationship between team members and helps reweave the "team fabric" that gets tattered and frayed in the course of day-to-day decision-making. For example, if your team collectively decided to eliminate one of your programs in order to cut costs, you would take it personally, even if you believed their decision was motivated by a genuine business need. Your response would be "Why *me*? Why *my* program?"

This human tendency to connect ourselves with what we do is behind the anger, frustration, despair, and/or resentment when collective decisions don't go our way. The bridging process enables people to separate themselves from what they do. When this happens, it is easier to "go along" with team decisions. More importantly, the members of your team then remain unified. Bridging becomes a team maintenance tool.

INDICATORS That Bridging Is Needed

A definitive list of indicators for the bridging initiative can get long. Most signs are in the form of conflict and resistance, from passive aggressive to overtly aggressive. The indicators for bridging range from a covert lack of cooperation to physically aggressive behavior.

Many experts agree that the majority of interpersonal communication is nonverbal, and that's particularly true with regard to differences of opinion. The fact that most of your team members will express disagreement with the team's decision nonverbally, or indirectly, makes it difficult to know when bridging is indicated. That's why the formal or structured alignment process intentionally includes two steps that help you zero in on those people you need to reach.

❑ If during the alignment process you hear clear statements of disagreement—for example, if someone says, "I can't go along with this decision,"—hear it as a demand for bridging.

The majority of the time, if individuals clearly say they disagree, they are inviting efforts to change their minds. Contrary to how it may appear, a clear statement of disagreement is a good sign. It demonstrates a desire to discuss the issue openly and offers a greater possibility of reaching alignment. Covert or nonverbal expressions of disagreement during the alignment process usually indicate that there is a wide gap that needs to be bridged between the team and the individual. These can include such behavior as:

❑ Vague statements in which an individual's position on the issue is not clear.

❑ A refusal or reluctance to speak and state a position.

❑ A third party telling you that one of the team members is having a problem with the team's decision. Sometimes people intentionally use an intermediary to let you know they disagree.

❑ An expression of agreement quickly followed with a "but if" statement.

For example, a common way people express disagreement is to create a dilemma. They do this by seeming to agree, but they go on to state how the action will create problems. They might say, for example, "I think we should open our stores earlier on Sunday . . . but if we do, we're going to have problems with the unions and local church leaders. We may even be facing a boycott." There's a difference between pointing out pitfalls around a decision and trying to shoot it down. That difference lies in the way concerns are expressed. If opinions are expressed as facts, events that *will* happen rather than events that *might* happen, it's likely a cover for an unexpressed personal disagreement.

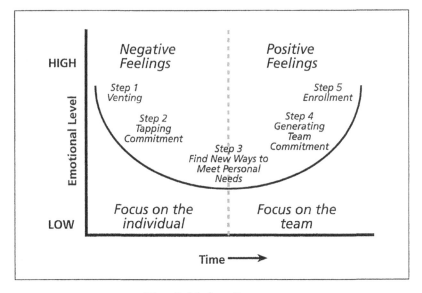

The Bridging Process

❏ Unfinished thoughts or individuals who say they are struggling for "the right words" are sometimes indications that you should initiate a bridging process to get at the underlying cause of the hesitation and reluctance of the individual.

The Bridging PROCESS

As you did with alignment, you may already be intuitively using bridging techniques. However, without the aid of a structured process, intuitive bridging can show up as coercion. Properly handled, bridging transforms potentially negative emotional feelings into positive energy. It is a form of coaching. Typically, you would conduct the following five-step bridging process in a one-on-one conversation. The Bridging Process graphic illustrates the movement resulting from the five-step process.

As you see in the graphic, each of the five basic steps of the bridging initiative moves a person from a negative to a positive emotional state, and from focusing on themselves to focusing on the team. By exploring personal feelings and needs first, people become more willing and able to consider team needs, often seeing previously unseen benefits to themselves in the process. This first focus on individual attention improves interpersonal relationships while still maintaining strong individual accountability.

The five steps in the bridging process are as follows:

Step 1—Venting emotion

Ask the individuals how they *feel* about the aligned decision. If you aren't sure whether bridging is needed, this step should make it clear. While sharing feelings may seem uncomfortable at first, you'll be surprised at what happens when you create an opening and listen. Venting makes room for the new possibilities that will turn up during your conversation. In general, people must say what they think and where they stand *before* they can listen.

Step 2—Tapping the commitment behind the feelings

By listening and asking a few simple questions, you will be able to get in touch with an individual's commitment. Questions such as "Where does that feeling come from?" or "What makes you say that?" are useful. The objective here is to allow people to reveal the beliefs, needs, and commitments behind their resistance to alignment. Often the beliefs, needs, and commitments of the individual and the team are the same and only the *means* of attaining them differ. If so, pointing out this area of agreement can bring the individual quickly into alignment. However, if there is a genuine difference, knowing the root cause of the resistance reveals new options and opportunities.

Step 3—Finding new ways to satisfy an individual's personal needs within the decision of the team

This step in the bridging process is really a facilitated brainstorming session in which you look for ways to satisfy personal needs while also staying within the arena of the actions the team intends to take. Polar thinking is often behind an individual's resistance to a team decision. The thinking is, "Either the team gets what it wants, or I do." So much time is spent resisting and defending positions, that there is little left to find a win/win solution. The bridging initiative provides "time out" so individuals can break out of the either-or thinking patterns.

Step 4—Generating commitment to the team decision

This step strongly reinforces the idea that team relationships are just as important as any single decision. One way to do this is to help the person you are trying to align compare both the *costs and benefits* of going along with the team's decision. The costs tend to be obvious because they are the reasons this individual disagrees. To get a handle on the costs, you have but to ask, "Why do you feel the team's decision is bad?" Make a list of their reasons and label the list "costs."

Once individuals have exhausted the reasons for disagreeing, ask, "What might be some of the benefits, if we implemented the team's decision?" They will undoubtedly struggle to answer, so be patient. Eventually, and with a little help from you, they will begin to identify benefits. Record their responses. Be sure that "maintaining personal relationships with the team" is on the list. Once the two lists are complete, with both "costs" and "benefits," share and discuss them with the individual.

Any course of action is seldom totally right or wrong. People weigh the costs and benefits—to their organization and themselves—and then go in the direction where there appears to be the greatest overall or long-term benefit. Step 4 simply shifts weight from the "costs column" toward the "benefits column" to make it more likely the individuals will be able to go along with the team's decision.

Step 5—Enrolling the individual in the aligned decision

Enrollment is a technique that can be used in conjunction with a variety of leadership initiatives, particularly alignment. In this context, the word enrollment is not a euphemism for "selling." Selling involves giving reasons why someone should want what you want. Enrollment allows individuals to see that they can meet their larger needs by going along with the team's decision. In short, selling emphasizes *your* needs; enrollment focuses on theirs. To conduct an enrollment conversation during the bridging process, ask the individual the following three questions:

- What factors do you think were motivating the team's decision?

This question gets the individuals in touch with the fact that there are business reasons for the decisions, and that they need not take the team's decision personally.

- How would you assess for yourself the "costs" and "benefits" of going along with the team's decision?

This question relates to Step 4 and is intended to get the individual to openly acknowledge that there are legitimate benefits to going along with the team's decision.

- Are you willing and able to go along with the team decision?

Listen closely to the answer. You want to hear expressed reasons for not aligning with the team, or get agreement to support the team's decision. Non-answers such as, "I'll think about it," or "We'll see," or "I'll do what I can," are not acceptable.

If individuals continue to disagree, regardless of the reason, you need to respond with the question, "What will it take for you to go along with the decision?" Negotiate and see if you can reach agreement on what adjustments you can make to the team's decision. As you recall, the alignment process itself left the door open to such adjustments.

If individuals agree to support the team's decision, quickly and concisely reiterate what they said they would do in a way that brings closure to the conversation and lets them know you are holding them accountable. Promise to touch base with them in the future to discuss any difficulties they may be having with the aligned decision or to identify any new concerns that may come up. This leaves the door open for further discussion so the individual doesn't feel trapped by this process.

Depending on your leadership style, bridging can be easy or difficult. How effective the five-step bridging process is depends on your natural tendencies. The coaching below provides additional tips on how to improve your natural bridging ability.

Your NATURAL ABILITY for Bridging

Bridging is one of the more difficult processes to distinguish, understand, and use. The bridging initiative can easily get distorted into some form of political maneuvering, bribery, or *coercion*. The advice set forth in this section can keep the bridging from being manipulative. In many ways, the bridging initiative is the means to achieving what is commonly called "win/win decision-making." You and your team win by getting aligned action, and the individuals you are bridging to also win by getting their larger needs met in new ways. Most importantly, the organization—your employees, customers, and shareholders—win because your leadership team is able to make quick decisions and follow through with decisive action.

◆ Bridging for the COMMANDER

Natural Ability Index: 5

Bridging involves an appreciation that emotional issues sometimes have to be dealt with in order to achieve a goal. As a Commander, you may view this notion as too vague or "touchy-feely," so bridging represents a definite leadership development opportunity for you.

To you, getting a direction to do something is sufficient reason to do it, so you may be struggling with the need for, and value of, bridging. On the other hand, your straightforward approach to difficult challenges and your need for quick, decisive action should enable you to see bridging's benefits. In fact practicing bridging may help change your reputation of being less than a team player.

It might be particularly difficult for you to see when bridging is needed and who needs it. To help move this kind of alignment along, however, fine-tune your perceptive apparatus to the more subtle, nonverbal forms of disagreement and conflict in your team or organization, because no one wants to take you head-on during the alignment process.

If you can make it through the first step of the bridging process, the venting step, the remaining steps will be easier. Venting requires listening. Don't turn it into a debate. You can feel the way you do and still let people feel the way they do, and discuss it.

♣ Bridging for the STRATEGIST

Natural Ability Index: 6

As a Strategist you are better at bridging than you give yourself credit for, so don't put it off. You will have more to worry about if you let it slide. The highly structured approach outlined in the Process section should help you get beyond your feeling that you shouldn't interfere. Bridging is a great way to show the *quiet power* that is the hallmark of your leadership style.

Your analytical skills and natural ability to see things clearly will give you the credibility needed to help your team weigh the costs and benefits of any decision objectively. You should share your unbiased perspective during the alignment process, and later on, use it in the five-step bridging process. Your nonjudgmental approach, coupled with your effectiveness in one-on-one conversations, can make you dynamite at bridging.

♥ Bridging for the COACH

Natural Ability Index: 5

At first blush, bridging may seem one of the easiest acts for you as a Coach to master, that is, it can be if you can get past one fairly big obstacle—your discomfort with difficult people. Bridging helps you overcome your tendency to reluctantly deal with problem people and difficult situations. While you may sense intuitively the need for bridging and who needs it, you may have difficulty getting started, but once under way, your natural ability will take over.

You are relatively comfortable dealing with emotional issues. That advantage, combined with your listening ability and need to get everyone on the team on board, gives you a leg-up when it comes to bridging. One word of warning: be careful during the venting step. Don't take a person's comments personally or overreact to criticism if some comes your way. Finally, during the six-step enrollment process, be more assertive, particularly during the last three steps. Holding people accountable is not only good for you and the team, but good for them, too. Maintaining personal accountability provides direction and more decisive, powerful, and effective action.

Bridging for the PERFORMER

Natural Ability Index: 7

Bridging is probably something you already do intuitively, part of your persuasive repertoire as a Performer. Your strong interpersonal skills, flexibility, and open mind make you particularly adept at this act. If you do encounter obstacles during the process, your ability to find creative solutions will serve you well, allowing you to keep and hold the alignment.

In terms of improving your bridging skills, I would offer three hints. First, guard against your tendency to dominate the conversation. Focus on the person you're bridging to. Second, make sure you're clear about the difference between selling and enrollment, otherwise you might slip into a selling mode. Finally, be sure to schedule and hold a follow-up session. Follow-up isn't your strong suit and some things may slip by you. It's time to change that. Hold people more accountable, including yourself.

Aligning and bridging help you to focus people's energy on making decisions. Once you're in action and making change, problems will naturally follow. The next pair of leadership initiatives deals with those breakdowns that inevitably occur once you begin to move toward your vision, goal, or objective.

INITIATIVE 7: MANAGING BREAKDOWNS
Keeping Action Going
When Things Get Tough

The previous two leadership initiatives, aligning and bridging, enable you to get your organization moving toward its vision. The next two initiatives, managing breakdowns and coaching, *keep* action going, even when circumstances and events try to slow or stop it. Managing breakdowns creates an organizational environment that supports the people in your organization as they relentlessly pursue your vision.

A breakdown is simply a stop in the flow of action. Managing a breakdown involves identifying and removing the barriers to cooperation and teamwork. These organizational barriers can be found in the type of reporting structure you have, the robustness of communication channels, as well as in policies and systems. Barriers to organizational cooperation also include cultural norms. For example, some organizations treat information as proprietary and don't share it widely. This makes it difficult for people within such an organization to cooperate and collaborate, because they simply don't know what's happening in the rest of their organization.

Many of the recent business trends focus on managing breakdowns and improving intra-organizational collaboration. For example, restructuring to reduce the number of management levels, as well as interventions like process reengineering serve to eliminate the barriers to organizational cooperation. Likewise, many businesses are changing their reward systems to focus less on individual contributions and more on accomplishment of team objectives and overall organizational performance. This approach, too, is an effort to remove barriers to cooperation and teamwork, and as such falls into the realm of managing breakdowns. Since a leader has responsibility for how the organization functions *as a whole,* it follows that managing breakdowns is a critical leadership initiative.

PURPOSE of Managing Breakdowns

The purpose of managing breakdowns is to identify and remove the barriers to cooperation within your organization, so people are encouraged and supported in their efforts to take action to address issues and problems as soon as they appear. Many organizations have structures, processes, and policies that make people hide, ignore, minimize, or undermanage problems. These barriers include a strong functional identity in which people identify more with their own particular department than with the total organization. Other obstacles take the form of performance reviews that emphasize individual performance, heavy reliance on chain-of-command, and hierarchical organizational structure.

As a leader, if you have successfully put the first six leadership initiatives into play, your organization is carving out a new future. And while that sounds exciting, creating a new and different future translates into *making change.* And, anytime you make change, you create "problems."

In most organizations, problems are seen as "bad." However, when you're leading an organization toward a new future, you are *intentionally* disrupting the status quo, and problems are to be expected. They come with the territory. For a leader, however, problems should not only be expected, but *welcomed*. For a leader, problems *should* be happening. Getting the rest of the organization to see problems that way, though, is not easy.

Solving problems is easier and faster if everyone in an organization cooperates, because problems have many causes, tend to be systemic, and involve several parts of an organization. For instance, late delivery to customers may seem like a problem in the shipping department, but the solution will likely involve other groups in the organization, such as production, sales, and possibly information systems. At some point representatives from all these functions will have to come together to solve the "late delivery" problem. How difficult or easy it is for them to do this will depend on your ability to remove the barriers to cooperation and teamwork—your ability to manage breakdowns.

Managing breakdowns is critical because if problems are ignored, minimized, and/or undermanaged, they will compromise your organization's performance, and ultimately the achievement of your vision. Unless you can quickly address breakdowns, your bold vision of the future will become an incremental improvement. Improvements in the range of five to ten percent aren't sufficient to meet market and shareholder expectations; and managing breakdowns is the key to creating results beyond "business as usual."

INDICATORS That Managing Breakdowns Is Needed

Unlike some of the other leadership initiatives, the indicators that managing breakdowns is needed are easy to spot. They show up first as angry and upset people and later as a decrease in the level of organizational performance. In general, when breakdowns occur, those people supporting the change that some see as causing the problems are attacked. Anytime you make change, two of the first things you encounter, after a period of shock and denial, are anger and resistance. Within an organizational context, this anger and resistance often show up as:

❑ Colleagues giving you "If it ain't broke, don't fix it" advice.

❑ A significant dip in employee morale that seems to indicate that planned changes are not working out.

❑ The formal or informal formation of coalitions of adversarial members of the management team.

❑ Operational dilemmas, in which traditional goals or standards are represented as being jeopardized by recent or planned changes.

In short, the triggers for managing breakdowns show up as people struggling, sometimes even fighting fiercely, to maintain the status quo. These attacks, arguments, and dilemmas are stressful and waste organizational energy. You may find yourself hesitating or pulling back from your intended goal or beginning to doubt the feasibility of your vision and goals—this hesitation being but another indicator that managing breakdowns is needed.

If the call for dealing with such breakdowns is not heeded, and the lack of organizational cooperation and teamwork leaves business problems without quick solutions, then the indicators become more severe. You might see a decline in your major measures of productivity and efficiency, like sales, revenues, and customer satisfaction. They may also show up on the bottom-line results like net income and rate of business growth. Of course, the object is to act *before* this happens, and initiate the managing breakdowns process before the bottom line is affected.

The Managing Breakdowns PROCESS

Cooperation and teamwork are at the heart of changing your people's relationship to problems. If you team people up for the purpose of solving a "problem," problems are transformed from something that "shouldn't be" to something that "should be expected." They become the team's reason for being. Some organizations understand this intuitively, creating a multitude of small teams (functional, inter-functional, and ad hoc) to solve problems. However, a leader must look at teaming on an even larger scale, seeing the organization as one large team. If the entire organization functions as one entity, then, as with smaller problem-solving teams, the organization's reason for being can be to solve problems, rather than to deny and avoid them.

Managing breakdowns identifies and removes the barriers that keep an organization from functioning as one team. While there are often dozens of such barriers in any organization, three areas that merit your special attention include:

- How profit and loss (P & L) responsibility is shared in your organization;
- How you measure performance, particularly financial performance;
- How your broad organizational structure and reporting relationships operate.

P & L responsibility is a necessary part of managing a business, but *how* it is shared is critical to facilitating and maintaining intra-organizational cooperation. In most cases, dividing up P & L among regions, divisions, or plants often promotes internal competition and leads to wasted energy and resources. It needn't be that way, however. Financial performance objectives among upper management and profit sharing are familiar examples of ways to divide and distribute P & L to encourage cooperation.

With regard to **performance measures,** an over-emphasis on near-term financial indicators, coupled with the blaming that inevitably ensues when the results are below expectations, creates a "pass the buck" mentality among people in your organization. Everyone is so busy dodging the blame for poor performance, no one focuses on the problem. In addition, when the blame finally falls in someone's lap, the response is to get rid of the person, believing that a person (or people) are solely responsible—which is seldom the case. This propensity to act impulsively, coupled with the lack of cooperation from teammates struggling to distance themselves from the problem, results in symptomatic relief only. The root cause(s) of the problem(s) cannot be addressed because the solution usually involves more than one group, department, or function. Balancing near-term financial reports with other longer-term indicators of progress toward the vision is one way to manage breakdowns.

Functional organizational structure is a barrier to co-operation and teamwork. Flurries of reengineering efforts are an indication that many organizations already recognize that organizing an enterprise around traditional business tasks, such as marketing, engineering, and operations, tends to isolate, rather than integrate, people and business activities. Process reengineering can be an effective way to dismantle functional structures, if not used simply as a facade for expense reductions or layoffs.

Narrowly defined jobs are often part of a functional organization structure, and are also a barrier to organizational cooperation. Basically, the smaller the scope of people's jobs, the more difficult it is for the people holding those jobs to see an organization's prob-lems as *their* problem. Giving people a narrow range of activities, choices, and responsibilities contributes to their feeling that they have little or no control over organizational performance. When employees *mentally abdicate* responsibility for organizational performance, overall organizational performance declines because employees begin doing even more work that doesn't have bottom-line impact and support the organizational vision. Decreasing the number of job levels and increasing the scope of jobs facilitate breakdown management because more people share the same set of problems as well as accountability for organizational performance.

These are just three areas you can explore as part of your larger managing breakdowns effort. In general, as organizations grow and evolve, they need to become more cooperative and collaborative. Often the opposite happens. So, as you add more people, functions, departments, processes, and systems, be careful that you are not creating barriers to cooperation and collaboration. This takes elegant design.

The more people function as members of one large team, the easier it is to focus organizational energy on finding and solving problems. Each problem addressed in a timely manner is a stepping-stone to making the organization's vision a reality.

Your NATURAL ABILITY for Managing Breakdowns

You can't survive long in today's business environment without being able to manage breakdowns, so it represents an area of development that can pay big dividends. The following tips for your leadership style will further enhance your ability to manage breakdowns more effectively.

◆ Managing Breakdowns for the COMMANDER

Natural Ability Index: 6

Since you tend, as a Commander, to be demanding with regard to performance results and standards, employees and colleagues may be slow to bring problems to your attention, fearing you'll see their report as an indicator of poor personal performance. Your tendency to be judgmental only adds to this dilemma. Logically you know now that problems are good, that they point to what isn't working, helping you keep things on track. However, you must dramatically change your initial, natural reaction of anger and blame. If you show appreciation to people who surface problems, and focus on the problem rather than finding fault, problems will surface earlier while they have less impact and are more easily managed.

As your Natural Ability Index suggests, to some degree, you are adept at managing breakdowns. Your orientation toward the future, coupled with your willingness to take risks and responsibility, allows you to hold firm to your vision. In the face of adversity, re-evaluation or self-doubt don't normally occur to you.

Finally, teaming is not your preferred *modus operandi*, because teams seem to imply a loss of control. Keep in mind that what you want and need is *accountability*, not control. While your control-oriented behavior may have served you well in the past, it may be keeping you from *superior* organizational performance in the future. If you really want to lead your organization beyond good or average performance, you must find new ways to maintain individual accountability. One of the best ways is to develop performance contracts with employees, much as you would if they were outside contractors.

♣ Managing Breakdowns for the STRATEGIST

Natural Ability Index: 7

For someone who isn't crazy about change to begin with, once you do commit to accomplishing a business goal, you can be dauntless. Your highly tuned perceptive abilities allow you, as a

Strategist, to be among the first to see problems on the horizon. If so, don't hesitate. Speak up. If you're worried about being seen as someone who is throwing cold water on an effort, learn to couch your concerns in a way that clearly shows you're committed to making things work.

As problems seem to pile up, your worrisome nature can get the better of you. However, once you start taking action to solve these problems, you are the best. Your powers of analysis are a great asset in managing breakdowns because you are able almost intuitively to find the root cause of problems.

While you may prefer to work alone or in small groups, don't let your preference for doing everything yourself interfere with the need to create a more unified organizational team. As noted earlier in the Process section, your focus must be on removing barriers to teamwork on an organizational level. This doesn't mean that you have to change the way you work personally, although it wouldn't hurt you to work more collaboratively.

♥ Managing Breakdowns for the COACH

Natural Ability Index: 2

Managing breakdowns is obviously one of the most challenging leadership initiatives for you. This is not because you don't have the natural ability to manage breakdowns, but rather because you tend to avoid conflict. You are particularly sensitive to personal attacks. Accept that anytime you make changes—even those to improve cooperation—you will hear criticism. When this happens, see these attacks as a positive sign indicating that fundamental changes are beginning to take hold in your organization.

If you can develop a new attitude about problems, managing breakdowns could well become your strong suit. You are a natural peacemaker, which is one way to think of this initiative. Let this and your natural appreciation of teamwork work for you. Knock down those organizational barriers to teaming, balancing business needs with human needs. From a business standpoint, you need to maintain accountability, which is more difficult for you. As you dismantle the barriers to teaming, remember that teams must be held accountable for delivering specific results.

Managing Breakdowns for the PERFORMER

Natural Ability Index: 1

Managing breakdowns is no fun for you at all. A Performer would much rather have someone else handle this leadership initiative. When problems surface, however, don't delegate. Your lack of personal involvement with problem-solving efforts can undermine your credibility with others in the organization. Often, your overall light-hearted approach to even serious business problems, while emotionally healthy, tends to be interpreted by some of your colleagues as a sign that you lack business savvy.

Managing breakdowns is about following through on your vision and related initiatives. It is about keeping action going in the face of adversity. Your persuasive ability can help you, but you need to do more, not just say more. For you, perseverance and follow-through represent an arena for growth and development.

INITIATIVE 8: COACHING

Improving Confidence in People's Ability to Perform

Complements Managing Breakdowns

Coaching is not advice, therapy, or cheerleading. Volumes have been written on coaching, mine being but one. My definition for coaching can be condensed into a sentence: coaching is a conversation designed to increase a person's confidence in their ability to perform. Coaching conversations can happen between any two people, or even between a person and a group or team. In a business organization, you can coach your peers, your subordinates, or even your customers. Ideally, there are no hard and fast rules as to who can coach and who can be coached, but there is one important prerequisite: coaching must be "invited."

While coaching is useful in many circumstances, it is a necessary adjunct to the managing breakdowns initiative, because once *external* barriers to an objective have been identified and addressed, coaching is needed to dismantle the *internal* barriers limiting performance.

If you were to ask people *what* leaders do, the majority would at least mention motivation. A leader motivates people. If you go on to ask *how* leaders motivate, you would get various vague and nebulous answers, such as "by inspiring people," "using charisma," or "connecting with people." So, if you really want to know how to motivate people, learn about coaching. Coaching moves people from "have to" to "want to."

PURPOSE of Coaching

As a leader, moving your organization toward a new vision or objective, by definition, changes the status quo. This change creates resistance that shows up as a host of problems. In some cases, these problems can seem insurmountable, prompting you or others to give up, or set your sights lower. The gap between your vision and the current reality can appear too big. It takes courage to step into that gap. So, coaching allows people and teams to take that crucial step. In the face of adversity, coaching keeps people mobilized.

Most organizations today attempt to keep going in the face of adversity via control—simultaneously promising reward and threatening punishment (i.e., you'll get a promotion if you do a good job, and you're fired if you screw up). While this "carrot and stick" approach can garner *compliance,* it does not create the kind of powerful committed action that coaching can deliver. Without coaching, people give what's necessary to get rewarded and/or avoid punishment. At the most, you get what you ask for. Coaching allows you to get everything people have to give.

INDICATORS That Coaching Is Needed

Indicators that the coaching initiative is needed typically masquerades as complaints or statements expressing anger or hopelessness. Unless you are familiar with coaching, you might respond with words of advice or consolation, when coaching is indirectly being requested. Indeed, that's one barrier that keeps coaching from getting a foothold in business organizations today: people do not know they can and should *request* coaching. So, be alert for *indirect* requests for coaching. For instance, some complaints are requests for coaching, while some are not. To tell the difference between a simple complaint and a hidden request for coaching, listen for *commitment*. If, in the complaint you hear or sense a strong commitment to act, coaching is indirectly being requested. In this case, you might offer coaching—maybe even use that term. If they're just letting off steam, chalk it up to *recreational complaining* and listen politely (or don't).

Other events or circumstances, which indicate that coaching is needed by you, or someone else in your organization, include:

❑ Serious consideration being given to substantial compromise on a business goal or some aspect of the organization's vision;

❑ Talk of abandoning a critical project or program entirely;

❑ Doubting whether you or another have the ability to achieve a result you/they previously committed to;

❑ Feeling alone in your/their commitment to a business objective;

❑ Admitting that, although still committed to the vision, goal, or objective, you/they cannot see any possibility for achieving it.

Fortunately, once an individual, team, and organization have a clear understanding of coaching, and once it is embedded in an organization, people request coaching. When you, your team, and /or your organization reach this stage of development, the coaching process takes off. This is because one's awareness of needing coaching automatically puts you/them in touch with your/their commitment to achieve the goal. That's important because it is human commitment that gives coaching its awesome power.

The Coaching PROCESS

Before coaching someone, you'll need to first meet certain conditions. When a breakdown occurs, people get upset. When an individual or team is in a highly charged emotional state, coaching should be delayed. If someone requests coaching while they are upset, then listen, maybe let them vent or leave them alone, but don't coach them. Begin coaching after they've cooled off. Coaching is an intellectual process that should take place after their emotions have settled down.

Secondly, coaching should be requested. Since requests for coaching are often disguised as complaints, you may need to restate their complaints, almost word for word, and add, "Would you like some coaching?" Once permission is received, and the person is listening, coaching can begin. One reason you ask for permission is simply to get the complainant to understand that this is a conversation with a purpose, not idle chatter.

Coaching should not masquerade as advice, consolation, or chitchat. Although coaching is a conversation, the coach primarily listens and poses questions, with the goal being to enable the person being coached to see his or her own way past the breakdown. An effective coaching conversation that manages breakdowns progresses in four steps:

Step 1—Isolating the facts

Upon encountering a problem, people immediately apply an interpretation. For example, one company leader whom I coached was Marie, the vice-president of public affairs for a Midwest utility company. The second time the senior management team canceled a critical meeting with Marie, it caused a breakdown for her. Marie interpreted the cancellation as evidence that the senior team, and its formal leader, did not support her new program. Since I was hired as an "outside" coach, I could quickly move into a coaching mode by asking, "What are the facts? What actually happened?" After considerable conversation, during which I asked the same questions several times, Marie realized that the cancellation may not have been as big a problem as she had thought. There were valid and reasonable explanations for the delay in reviewing her proposed program, which had nothing to do with how well her program or she was liked or valued. Separating fact from the coachee's interpretation often resolves much of the breakdown.

Step 2—Getting in touch with the original commitment

A coach is only as strong as the commitment of the individual being coached. Coaching requires commitment. Continuing with Marie's problem, I shifted the conversation to help her get in touch with her original commitment by asking her, "Why is this program important to you?" As she answered, Marie got back in touch with the reason she took it on in the first place. As she spoke, her voice, body, and words took on a new energy. "Let me at 'em!" Marie finally said, and we were ready to talk about other options.

By the way, if it becomes clear that individuals are no longer committed to their objective, the coaching conversation should end and the discussion shift to finding ways to get out of the situation that's causing concern and stress. Coaching and commitment must go hand in hand. When commitment goes, so does the possibility for coaching.

Step 3—Finding other ways forward

Problems can seem overwhelming when there are only a few options or possible solutions. Therefore, a necessary part of coaching conversations involves generating a list of possible actions. It's like brainstorming, but the coach makes few, if any, suggested actions. With Marie, I may have said something like, "Marie, what are some ways you could nail down a meeting with the senior team?" and "Is it possible to review your proposed program as part of another meeting, rather than requesting a separate one?" This approach would help Marie discover previously unseen ways forward.

Step 4—Getting a promise to act

Once the coaching conversation generates a sufficient list of possibilities to deal with the problem, you should shift the conversation to selecting the one(s) with the most potential. The person being coached must make the choice. It is sometimes desirable to pursue two or three courses of action or take action with a "fall-back" course in mind.

You close the coaching conversation by getting a clear and specific commitment to act, what action will be taken and when. Coaching conversations always end with the individual posed to take action. You may now state your intention to follow up, to find out how the new tack fared. This offer continues your coaching relationship and adds a critical point of accountability.

Your NATURAL ABILITY for Coaching

The introduction and practice of coaching has great potential to transform an organization and its culture because it provides an effective way to motivate people and maintain accountability. Coaching offers a beneficial alternative to controlling behaviors, processes, and policies. Over time it changes the culture of an organization by changing fundamental mindsets about what motivates people, about problems, and about what is and isn't possible in the organization.

◆ Coaching for the COMMANDER

Natural Ability Index: 1

You may see yourself as a coach, but more like the type standing on the sidelines calling plays, not the one having a conversation in the locker room. Logically coaching should have great appeal for you, since it helps you to motivate people into action. While you have other ways to accomplish this, your control-oriented approach often creates resistance, hurt feelings, and half-hearted efforts.

One good opportunity to test your newfound coaching skills might be if you have to deal with an employee who missed a critical deadline. Instead of blowing your top and tightening the screws, try a coaching conversation. Follow the four steps: Ask the individual what happened. Determine if this person has a real commitment to completing the task. If so, help generate at least three or four different ways the individual could complete the project and at the same time maintain your confidence and trust. Finally, ask the person to select one or more of the possibilities and promise to take action. Then stand back. You'll see that this coaching technique delivers better results than a command and control approach.

Your direct and honest manner, together with your natural appreciation for straight talk, will serve you well because coaching is not an emotional process. It's logical and orderly. Just try to curb your tendency to decide for the coachee. The last thing someone being coached needs is your opinion.

Perhaps for you the most difficult part of mastering this leadership initiative is just getting started. You might tend to see those who need and request coaching as weak. Your leadership development will take a critical turn as you learn to distinguish between weakness and vulnerability. One of the most powerful things leaders can do is to share their own vulnerability. You're usually up for taking a risk, so go for it!

♣ Coaching for the STRATEGIST

Natural Ability Index: 5

As a Strategist, you'll often see the need for coaching before others do. Your insight is a valuable contribution to people and teams that are beginning to appreciate and use coaching. Within the initiatives managing breakdowns and coaching, maybe you can see a way for teams to be more open to your mostly helpful criticism. It is not uncommon for people to ask your advice, since you are a thoughtful and objective person. The next time someone asks for your counsel, try coaching. Begin by asking if he or she would like some *coaching* (begin to use that term). Let the four-step process be your guide. You will almost intuitively move through the first three steps. Remember, though, the individual develops the possibilities for action and chooses the one(s) to act on. Keep your coaching conversations as short as possible and remember Step 4. Your need to be thorough and avoid mistakes might make it difficult for you to move someone into action after only a brief conversation, but trust the process.

Your clear analytical thinking, logical and unemotional demeanor, and your relative comfort in one-on-one conversations will make you an expert coach. Coaching is one way for you to deal with your hesitation to take action. So the next time you find yourself hesitating to act, request some coaching yourself. Every good coach is coachable.

♥ Coaching for the COACH

Natural Ability Index: 10

Obviously, this is your forte because you already coach intuitively, if not formally. Your supportive nature, ability to stay calm in a crisis, and your patience and compassion make coaching comfortable for you. If there is one word of caution, it would be to keep your emotional distance from those you are coaching. A coach cares, but is not a caretaker.

For instance if, in the midst of a coaching session, an individual decided to confront the boss with a concern, you might be tempted to offer to accompany that person or possibly even approach the boss on that individual's behalf. Don't do it. Remember that coaching is a learning and confidence-building tool and *people have to do it themselves.*

And a final bit of coaching . . . remember Step 4. Coaching results with people taking action. It's not only a "feel-good" endeavor. People must know you're holding them accountable for doing what they promised to do.

♠ Coaching for the PERFORMER

Natural Ability Index: 2

You may think that a Natural Ability Index ranking of 2 is off-base for you as a Performer. It may well be . . . or it may be that you're confusing advising or counseling with coaching. Your natural ability to see solutions, coupled with your persuasive powers, makes you an excellent *advisor*. A coach doesn't focus on solutions, actions, or results per se, but rather the success of the individual they're coaching. I sometimes tell clients that I couldn't care less about their goal, but that I do care about their success. Seeing that difference is the first step to mastering the coaching initiative and a very important one for you to develop as a Performer.

Coaching, by definition, involves keeping things going. Obviously you're better at getting them started. You are the instigator of many successful programs and are always looking for opportunities to break new ground. How about being the first to institute a coaching development program? But, if you decide to do it, follow through. Learning to put as much interest and energy into a program *after* it is under way would be a valuable leadership lesson. A coaching program might provide that opportunity.

The first eight initiatives are focused on building and maintaining a vital organization. Logic might suggest that the leadership cycle ends here. However, no organization is able to sustain growth *indefinitely* by simply becoming bigger and better. There comes a time in the history of every organization when it begins to crumble under its own weight. It becomes too large, too diversified, or too narrow in scope to compete effectively. If it is to survive it must *reinvent itself*, as though it were just going into business today. Essentially, this is the focus of the last two leadership initiatives—renewing and acknowledging accomplishment.

INITIATIVE 9: RENEWING

Tearing Down and Reinventing Your Enterprise

Renewing is the process of "starting over"—beginning a new business using the assets of your existing business: capital, customer base, reputation, physical plant, and people. In most cases renewing actually involves tearing down most or part of your existing organizational structure, redesigning processes, and acquiring new knowledge and skills, at the most advantageous time.

While there are many circumstances that might drive a leader to renew, almost all catalysts for renewal involve a decline in the rate of growth. Simply put, the business cannot continue to grow the way it is structured and/or focused. For example, the renewal of a consumer electronics manufacturer was stimulated by a declining trend in its rate of growth. Revenues sank to a 3 percent annual rate of growth from an average of 10 percent in previous years.

At first the company tried to compensate in such ways as increasing production, redesigning the manufacturing process, and establishing quality circles. While those efforts resulted in slight improvements, their impact was temporary. The company was seemingly operating at peak efficiency, yet its rate of growth continued to decline. The only way to grow the business was to literally get into a new business, so this consumer electronics company transformed itself from a sub-assembly operation to an end-to-end manufacturer. It now manufactures 70 percent of all the components it utilizes, whereas it used to assemble larger components, using parts from other suppliers.

Renewal for this electronics firm involved moving its operations to a bigger site, purchasing and relocating two small manufacturing businesses to its new location, creating a partnership with a trucking firm, restructuring its management team, and doubling the number of employees. Within two years after implementing their renewal, the number of customers tripled because the company was able to compete and sell its products overseas. Its rate of growth reached double digits again. That's renewal.

Without the renewing initiative, this company would have likely been stuck in a mode of trying to compensate for the decline in growth. Their initial reaction was to manage their way out of the situation, by adding new shifts and quality circles. Indeed, in business today, the tendency is to manage out of every problem. You can't do that with large systemic problems like a continuing market share decline or accelerating overseas competition. Management solutions can only take a company so far; then leadership initiatives must take over. Renewal is one of those initiatives.

As the last of the core leadership initiatives, renewing is the hallmark of leadership. It involves casting aside what may be mostly working, to create something that will ensure success in the future. In the end leadership is about making change a *choice*, rather than a chance. Renewal ultimately becomes the most critical choice a leader makes.

The PURPOSE of Renewing

Renewing ensures an organization's sustained growth. It requires purposefully beginning the leadership cycle again by initiating an envisioning process at the right time. How often renewal is needed varies greatly, and is dependent on your type of business, the competitive forces, and the overall efficiency of your operation. A large electric utility might renew about every 50 years, while a computer software company might engage in a renewal effort every 10 years. Whatever the interval, renewing is inevitable. Without it, your organization will naturally decline, and as it does, it becomes increasingly subject to the external forces of change. This reactive mode hastens the demise of your enterprise and increases the urgency for its renewal.

Renewing can change from a competitive advantage to a survival tactic if it is delayed. However, when executed at the proper time, it is proactive in nature and provides a competitive advantage. The old saying about a good offense being the best defense is true when it comes to renewal.

From an emotional standpoint, renewing is the most difficult leadership initiative to perform because it involves tearing down some or most of what you, and others, have labored hard to build. Most leaders logically understand that change is easier to manage when you make the change, but that doesn't make renewing any easier. You can get frozen in a self-made dilemma concerning when to start over, caught between the logical signs calling for renewal (in the Indicators section), and your own emotional feelings. Psychologically, there never seems to be a good time to renew.

Because a company usually tries to manage its way out of its decline in growth, the optimum time for renewal usually comes at a time when the organization is in turmoil. The whole group of employees is trying to catch its collective breath after instituting reengineering, restructuring, lay-offs, quality programs, and/or other such efforts. Understandably, the thought of subjecting the organization to a renewal effort becomes emotionally abhorrent. But it must not be put off when it is needed.

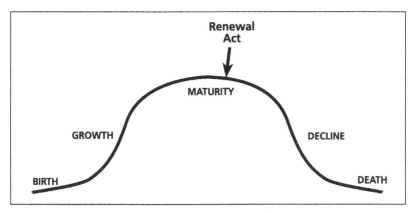

Initiating Renewal

Even though it always seems to take place in somewhat of a quagmire, the renewing initiative is the shortest one to carry out time wise, because the decision to renew can happen in the wink of an eye. However, implementing renewal, which begins with the first leadership initiative, envisioning, can mean many months of effort—sometimes a year or more. It's a big commitment. As such it's not surprising that renewal triggers many of the requests I receive for coaching.

INDICATORS That Renewing Is Needed

When asked *when* to initiate the renewing, I often say, "Before you want to." However, such smart-aleck remarks aren't very helpful. You need observable indicators that renewing is called for. Renewing should occur as soon as a sustained decline in the *rate* of growth is apparent. Everything in our world follows a predictable life cycle, a symmetrical, bell-shaped curve taking businesses, products, ideas, and all living things through a cycle from birth to decline and death. Renewal should occur just after the apex of this curve as shown in the Initiating Renewal graphic.

Because you don't want renewal to be triggered by a false aberration, make sure there is a clear downward *trend* in the rate of growth. How long that trend needs to be depends on the total length of the life cycle. A mathematical function called a logistic can tell you almost exactly how long maturity and decline will last. However, in general, the sooner you initiate renewing the better.

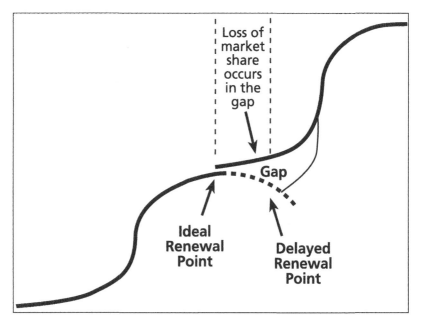

Renewal Gap

Looking at a life cycle in terms of *cumulative growth,* you can see that it becomes the familiar S-curve. Renewing at the top of the S-curve ensures optimal performance, using your organization's forward momentum to initiate a new growth cycle. If you delay renewal until your organization begins to decline, you will find that the initial growth curve is steeper, requiring more resources. The bigger problem is the loss in *time*. It is in the gap between optimal or ideal renewal and delayed renewal that competitors move in to take more market share. (See Renewal Gap graphic.)

These signposts will help you recognize when renewing is needed:

❏ For businesses, renewal should be initiated immediately after a sustained drop in the rate of growth is apparent.

❏ Another indicator that renewal is called for, and perhaps past due, is a recent influx of new competitors.

❏ Another common indicator is buy-out or take-over attempts, as competitors swoop in to eliminate competition and buy additional capacity at "discount prices."

Competitors are almost always able to see the need for renewal of your organization before you do, because they have none of your emotional baggage. For competitors, your need to renew shows up as an opportunity, a new market niche, or an unmet customer need. Competitors see your business ignoring a customer segment or missing an opportunity to supply a new product to your existing customers. They are counting on the fact that they can get into that market or create that product before you can act. Most of the time they're right, because established companies, which have experienced many years of growth and success, are reluctant to do anything as "revolutionary" as renewal. Most human beings hesitate when renewal is called for, because of the emotional pain and hard work that come with it.

Leaders cannot afford to engage in such delays. If you wait too long to renew, the indicators become meaningless, because they will show up in your annual financial statement and annual report. If this happens, it is too late to use renewal as a competitive advantage. You'll be in a survival mode. Poor financial performance, as well as unfriendly takeovers, the sale of company assets to meet earnings commitments, and other reactionary moves, might trigger what might be labeled renewal, but it will not be the proactive leadership act we were talking about here.

The Renewing PROCESS

The renewing initiative is less of a process and more of a decision that has three components:

- Knowing when to renew
- Making the decision to renew
- Removing the barriers to renewal

As simple as it sounds, not following these three steps have been the undoing of more than one leader.

Knowing when to renew—The optimal point to renew your organization may be at a time when there are no serious problems plaguing your enterprise. Although there may be a fall-off in the rate of growth, revenues and earnings seem acceptable. For this reason, your colleagues are likely to greet the suggestion to renew with, "If it ain't broke, don't fix it," and from a management point of view they're right. The focus of *management* is to keep production moving and on track. However, renewing is a *leadership* initiative, and the focus of leadership is to create *long-term* sustainable growth. The resistance you will feel when you begin to put the renewing initiative into play could be seen as a clash between leadership and management roles.

A new vision, which quickly follows on the heels of any renewal effort, must be compelling enough to overcome the people's tendency to want to manage their way out of current problems, rather than to face a more dramatic renewal effort.

However, even with a powerful vision, it is difficult to initiate renewal at the optimal time. For this reason, many organizations delay renewal efforts longer than they should. A delayed renewal initiative is easier to initiate, but more difficult to implement—and is far more dangerous to the organization, because competitors have usually had time to make inroads.

Making the decision to renew—If renewal is delayed, problems will be apparent, particularly the threat or onset of decreasing market share. Renewal is easier to initiate, but more difficult to implement properly because of the reactionary mindset delayed renewal tends to create. Delaying renewal puts you and your people in a survival mode, and our actions will tend to focus on the symptoms of decline (eroding market share, rising costs, etc.) rather than on the deeper underlying causes within the enterprise itself. When initiating a delayed renewal effort, creating a compelling vision—one that pulls rather than pushes—is even more critical.

Removing barriers to renewal—The last element of renewing involves addressing the mostly psychological and emotional barriers holding people back. From *inside* your organization, renewal can be seen as a veiled indictment, the unspoken message being, "What we're doing isn't good enough." or "What we've done doesn't count." For example, the plant manager of that consumer electronics company, cited earlier, was initially resistant to the plant relocation and to the merging of operations with a newly acquired company. While he used facts and figures to show how the inefficiency of having two new operations would hurt the company, the real reason he resisted showed up in a quiet one-on-one conversation, when he said: "This predicament was probably predictable. There was something I may have overlooked." He was saying that he felt like he had let the company down. He didn't do the right things, or didn't do enough to improve plant efficiency. He saw renewal as a sign of personal failure.

Many people will have a tendency to interpret renewal as either a failure on their part, a failure on senior management's part, or both. This issue must be addressed *directly* or people will not let go of the old ways, let alone buy into a new vision. A sense of personal failure is the primary reason managers and employees may resist, or even undermine, renewal efforts.

Clear communication is part of the answer for how to achieve effective renewal. Employees must hear that renewal is a natural evolutionary process, and that their hard work and dedication have positioned the enterprise well for renewal. Related to this, employees must be acknowledged for their past accomplishment, so the above message is seen as genuine.

Your NATURAL ABILITY for Renewing

Renewing can quickly become a divisive issue on any leadership team because style differences tend to put members in opposition regarding the need for this leadership act and/or its timing. Awareness of these natural differences will go a long way toward facilitating a dialogue leading to alignment on a proposed renewal.

◆ Renewing for the COMMANDER
─────────────────────────────

Natural Ability Index: 10

Commanders are ready, willing, and able to renew. Your acute awareness of current circumstances, combined with your overall future and action orientation, makes renewing second nature to you. Deciding to do it is easy because you're a risk taker and not heavily invested in the status quo. However, getting others enrolled—getting aligned action—is your challenge.

You may already have a reputation for being abrupt, moving ahead too quickly, and leaving others behind. Some of that may be deserved, but much of it has to do with your demeanor. While it would be a good general rule of thumb for you to use more finesse than force in most situations, you need to adopt this practice early on. For example, if indicators for renewal are present, control your tendency to take unilateral action and declare a restructuring, or search for a merger or strategic alliance. Rather, plant the seeds for renewal in one-on-one conversations with your direct reports and let the renewal conversation grow naturally until *others* suggest it.

In addition, you may have noted that while renewing is your forte, ranking a 10 on the Natural Ability Index, its complement, acknowledging accomplishment, is at the other end of the spectrum for you. The key to successful renewal for the Commander, lies in *how* you implement and support it.

♣ Renewing for the STRATEGIST

Natural Ability Index: 2

Your natural ability to notice trends in their embryonic stages makes you one of the first to notice the trend in a declining rate of growth—the primary indicator for renewal. However, as a Strategist you have a seemingly innate resistance to dramatic changes that may tempt you to manage your way out. The whole concept of renewal may seem to be reckless from your point of view, but, of course it is not, if it's managed properly and initiated in a timely manner.

Renewing is one time when you *should* let your intellect call the shots. The natural patterns, the life cycle, and related S-curve of renewing are intellectually undeniable. Your hesitation or resistance to act in a bold manner is the result of your innate dislike for chaos and wholesale change. One of the best ways to cope with the conflict between your intellect and psyche is to enlist the aid of others who would naturally be more inclined toward renewal. Seek out the Commanders and Performers on your team. Let their counsel, energy, and commitment support you, giving you the confidence you need to proceed. Since they ultimately will have to be enrolled in the process anyway, you might as well collaborate with them from the start.

♥ Renewing for the COACH

Natural Ability Index: 1

"Why does a coach only rate a score of 1 on the index?" you may be asking. In a word, "pain." Renewal in an organization is that part of the natural growth cycle that involves human pain. As a Coach, you tend to focus on the pain that renewal will create, rather than on the ultimate benefit it will bring to all people in the organization. Indeed, if the decision to renew is yours, your ongoing hesitation may delay it unnecessarily. Keep in mind that delaying renewal will ultimately cause *more* pain. If it is delayed too long, your organization will be put in a reactive mode, forcing layoffs, budget slashing, or downsizing.

Your awareness and concern for people will serve you and your organization when it comes to implementing renewal. However, you may need help getting started. Others on your team, the Commanders and Performers, will see the need and be advocating renewal long before you will. Listen to them. Renewing can be your "blind spot," so pay particular attention to the indicators and admonishments from colleagues.

♠ Renewing for the PERFORMER

Natural Ability Index: 8

Renewal has a natural appeal because of its core word—new. You know you're at your best when initiating a new effort, but be careful not to turn renewal into a program or event. It's an all-encompassing process, not a communications event.

During the process your persuasive powers will be put to the test, as many of your colleagues will be slow to climb on the "renewal bandwagon," the Strategists and the Coaches in particular. Each leadership style requires a different approach, and an enthusiastic hard sell won't work with those who hesitate or resist. Patient, one-on-one dialogues are what you need. Listen more . . . talk less.

Before you or anyone in your organization can grab onto something new, you must first let go of what you're already holding onto. This is often difficult. After all, if you're holding a pretty good poker hand, it may be difficult to discard part of it for the chance you may draw better cards.

Once the renewal effort is under way, you're entering a new cycle with an envisioning initiative, where your high energy and natural enthusiasm have free rein. It will really pay off during the implementation phase of renewal.

The last leadership initiative complements renewing by enabling people in your organization to let go of the old vision and reach for the new one.

INITIATIVE 10: ACKNOWLEDGING ACCOMPLISHMENT
Creating a Deep Sense of Fulfillment

Complements Renewing

Acknowledging accomplishment is an interpersonal communication process in which employees review the past achievements of their enterprise, recognize how they each *personally* contributed, and then are publically acknowledged by the leaders of their organization. The core message is: "You did well. Thank you." The objective of this initiative is to ensure that employees, and other stakeholders, feel valued. The outcome is the ongoing committed action of employees, leading to higher efficiency, creativity, and productivity.

Acknowledging accomplishment can be achieved by using ceremonies, video presentations, articles in the company newspaper, parties, etc. Almost any technique or combination of techniques can do the job, if it has two attributes. First, any techniques should be "public." Public means that the acknowledgment is witnessed by colleagues. Second, it must be initiated by, and include, the real and/or perceived leader(s) of an organization. That's what makes this a *leadership* initiative, and not just a "management technique."

The PURPOSE of Acknowledging Accomplishment

Accomplishment is not just the successful completion of a task, but the personal ownership of that success. Accomplishment is the coming together of both success and fulfillment. The Dynamics of Accomplishment graphic shows how success (measured in awards like promotions and bonuses) and fulfillment (measured in feelings of self-worth and self-confidence) should grow in tandem.

The concept of accomplishment is challenging to explore because it involves deep feelings. Although we tend to measure success in terms of tangible items like big homes and new cars, success is really a *feeling*. You might ask yourself if you are successful. As measured in tangible terms, you may say, "Yes." But now ask yourself, "Do I *feel* successful?"

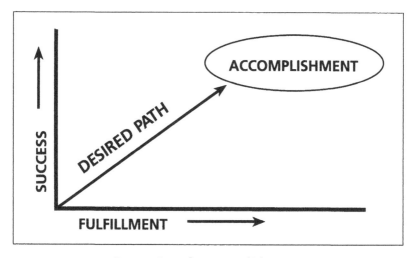

Dynamics of Accomplishment

Too often when I ask accomplished clients, and their employees, if they *feel* successful, they say, "not really." Yet, without a sense of accomplishment, people will only operate at a

137

minimal level—just enough to stay out of trouble. Obviously, this is not what you want in *any* business situation, but mediocre performance is deadly during a renewal effort. That's why acknowledging accomplishment complements renewal. Specifically, this initiative produces three outcomes that serve to support renewal.

1. It allows employees to let go of the past.

2. It ensures that the organization will operate at peak performance while in a vulnerable state of transition.

3. It helps ensure alignment on, and commitment to, the new vision that will be created as part of the renewal process.

With regard to the first point, you may recall that renewal is often perceived as a veiled indictment of failure. After all, the reasoning goes, why would you want to tear things down and rebuild, unless there is something wrong with what we've created?

Most managers and employees see their jobs as maintaining and improving production and/or services. Since renewing usually makes drastic changes in production and service delivery (i.e., reengineering, adding robotics, new computer systems, etc.), the natural assumption is that the old methods, and recent improvements, weren't good enough. Employees will understandably be upset if they are left to feel as though they wasted years of their life maintaining and improving a process, system, or operation that is being redesigned, or possibly even junked. Acknowledging accomplishment helps to put this notion to rest. It celebrates past successes, and in so doing, helps employees to let go of the past.

During the process of simultaneously tearing down the old, and rebuilding the new, an organization is extremely vulnerable. Maintaining quality, productivity, and customer service while in this state of flux requires both the good will and a high level of discretionary effort from employees. Projects and customers can slip through the cracks of newly designed processes, unless employees are willing and able to catch them. Acknowledging accomplishment maintains employee morale, which can suffer during times of change. More importantly it taps much-needed discretionary productivity. No company can operate at peak performance without it.

Finally, once their accomplishments are acknowledged, the employees are freer to commit to the new vision. If their personal contributions toward achievement of the previous vision have been acknowledged and appreciated, why wouldn't they want to support the new one as well? Bringing closure to, and letting go of the past, allows them to grasp the future. Acknowledging accomplishment ensures that employees not only go along with, but wholeheartedly *commit* to the new direction. Remember, committed people give everything they can, not just what they are asked for. While there are many factors that contribute to a successful renewal, none are more critical than acknowledging accomplishment.

INDICATORS That Acknowledging Accomplishment Is Needed

Because acknowledging accomplishment is fundamental to improving and maintaining human performance, when it is missing, it creates huge problems. Some of the indicators that acknowledging accomplishment is missing include:

- ❑ Low morale AND poor performance;
- ❑ Management continuity issues, e.g., unexpected requests for promotion and/or requests for transfer;
- ❑ Attacks on the new vision;

❑ Resistance to work additional overtime, when it had been accepted in the past.

When people don't get the acknowledgment they need, they find "creative" ways of asking for it. For example, indirect requests for acknowledgment can show up as a seemingly endless stream of people marching into your office, calling your attention to problems, and then briefing you on how they have *already* solved them or plan to solve them. Sound familiar? If so, you are being asked to acknowledge accomplishment. If they have already solved a problem or are about to do so, why are they coming to you? Answer: they want acknowledgement and praise. While their overt purpose may be to "keep you in the loop," you can bet that they also want and need an "atta boy" or "atta girl" from you.

Some skepticism and resistance to a new vision are to be expected, but widespread *attacks* on the new organization's vision are an indication that acknowledging accomplishment is needed. The old vision is incomplete until the organization has delivered on the promise of the old or previous vision, and this means that individuals within the organization know that *they* made it happen. This is a critical component of acknowledging accomplishment. Indeed, if the previous, or old, vision has been completed, and there are still widespread attacks and resistance to renewing, then acknowledging accomplishment is needed.

The Acknowledging Accomplishment PROCESS

Sometimes we confuse parties and ceremonies with acknowledgment. While they may be part of this initiative, public celebrations and acknowledging accomplishment aren't the same. Acknowledging accomplishment involves learning what happened and why it happened. This acknowledgement should be alluded to in widely broadcast communications, but it is important that it be handled in smaller groups.

At or near the conclusion of any endeavor, the group responsible and its leader should engage in a casual, but structured discussion. The focus of this discussion should be to uncover what happened, what worked, what didn't work, and why. Within this dialogue people become aware of what they need to do to improve personal and organizational performance. As a consequence of this dialogue, individuals and teams become aware that *they did it*—they made it happen. This awareness that they made it happen, coupled with the learning about what worked and what didn't work, assures you that these people will keep doing the things that worked, and stop doing the things that didn't. This is a simple concept and process, yet it seldom happens. The moment one project is completed, we rush on to the next, forgetting to take a thoughtful inventory of past accomplishments.

Think back to a time when you worked with a team and achieved a result beyond expectations. Ask yourself, or others on that team, how you did it. You'll often hear: "We were just at the right place at the right time," "Something just clicked," or "I'd have to give most of the credit to our team leader." These are examples of the tendency to *give away* acknowledgment. Even if this is just false humility, saying these words is disempowering. Most people are not truly aware of the contributions they make. Even if there is a vague sense of having made a difference, they often don't realize *exactly* what they did. With little or no awareness of having made a contribution, and without knowing exactly what that contribution was, it is impossible to replicate the performance. What is worse, good performers will not *want* to replicate it.

Acknowledging accomplishment must include everyone who contributed to an effort. All the participants must have the opportunity to *speak about their accomplishment*. It's absolutely essential that *they* speak. You cannot speak their accomplishment for them, although, unfortunately, leaders do it all the time. In a large organization, this process can be accomplished in small groups. Even in the largest organizations, these small dialogues can continue to expand, including more and more teams, until everyone who contributed is assembled together, physically or metaphorically. *Then* let the celebration begin!

The dialogue to acknowledge accomplishment is generally a group discussion—a collective, chronological reminiscence. Reminiscing is something we do intuitively, even ritualistically. You and your spouse may reminisce about your courtship on your wedding anniversary. Your family recalls Christmases past as they gather around the Yuletide dinner table. In large part, you do this to instill and feel a sense of accomplishment and foster unity,

Like most of the other leadership initiatives, acknowledging accomplishment is intuitive. Almost any speech you give to employees or shareholders inevitably includes a reference to your company's tradition of success, a litany of recent accomplishments, and some expression of personal pride and thanks. Learning to acknowledge accomplishment *intentionally, with an eye toward learning,* will raise you to a higher level of leadership performance, and embed the ritual of acknowledging accomplishment within your organization.

Your NATURAL ABILITY for Acknowledging Accomplishment

While there are many social and cultural practices about how to give and receive acknowledgment, your *style* ultimately determines your propensity toward giving acknowledgment, as well as the individual way you do it.

◆ Acknowledging Accomplishment for the COMMANDER

Natural Ability Index: 2

This initiative may seem a bit "overdone" from your perspective. Maybe you feel that people were "just doing their job" and really don't need acknowledging. Or maybe you're just anxious to get started on the next project. But people *do* need to be acknowledged, and that includes you. While you may take great solace in material gains, alone they can leave you unfulfilled.

Don't rush headlong onto a new project or into a new vision. If you charge forward in your inimitable manner, you will leave your people behind. Acknowledging accomplishment pays big dividends, and your primary responsibility with regard to this act is to make sure it happens. Your role in the process can vary. For example, a personal heartfelt letter from you addressed to each employee by name, or even a video presentation, can be used to kick off a series of learning dialogues among natural teams. If you are so inclined, you can preside over a gathering of all the teams, adding your personal acknowledgment to that which has been generated within small group discussions. In designing your own acknowledgment sessions, do whatever is comfortable and natural, just make sure all the contributors speak about their accomplishments (including you).

♣ Acknowledging Accomplishment for the STRATEGIST

Natural Ability Index: 3

Because acknowledging accomplishment is tied up with renewal and change, with which you tend to be uncomfortable, you may shy away from acknowledging accomplishment, too.

Although you intuitively go through the process of analyzing what worked, what didn't work, and why, you will tend to focus too much on what didn't work. Your need to be perfect, combined with your tendency to be critical, can make you focus on the "hole" rather than the "donut."

While you may not feel comfortable conducting or participating in small group discussions focused on accomplishment, you can arrange to keep your active role to a minimum. As a leader, just see that these discussions take place, perhaps letting others more comfortable in groups facilitate the acknowledging.

In these sessions, all individuals need the opportunity to speak their accomplishments, as do you. Curb your tendency to "give away" your accomplishment. And while you may feel out of place, it would be a growth experience for you to participate personally in most or all of the team discussions. Give it a shot.

Acknowledging Accomplishment for the COACH

Natural Ability Index: 8

Your unselfish nature, combined with your attention to people's needs, makes acknowledging accomplishment one of your strongest leadership acts. Just be careful not to give away *all* the accomplishments to others. You deserve some praise, too.

As you facilitate a look back over recent successes, don't see any discussion of "what didn't work" as criticism. And, when criticism shows up, don't take it personally. Making room for future improvement should not negate a sense of personal fulfillment.

Acknowledging Accomplishment for the PERFORMER

Natural Ability Index: 4

You'll be better at acknowledging accomplishment if you can manage two of your natural tendencies as a Performer. First, guard against taking over dialogues and discussions. While your intention may be to gain well-deserved acknowledgment for your contribution, your garrulous nature is often perceived as grabbing the limelight.

You are prone to confuse parties and other celebrations with the actual act of acknowledging accomplishment. Your playful nature and appreciation of fun are special gifts you bring to your organization. However, a party is only part of acknowledgment. There's a learning component, too. Simply arranging a team meeting and asking questions like: "Exactly what did you do?," "How did you do it?," "What worked?," "What would you do differently in the future?," and then adding a heartfelt "thanks," is all it takes. Sometimes a shorter discussion is preferable because it seems less contrived.

The Leadership Initiatives and More

Taken in turn, the ten initiatives form an overall leadership process, flowing from envisioning through renewing. The ease with which you execute these ten acts determines your overall leadership ability. Putting the entire process into play ensures the sustainable growth of your enterprise—the ultimate object of the leadership game.

Your innate leadership style predisposes you to recognize, value, and easily perform many of the ten leadership initiatives. Others you must develop and strengthen. The Natural Ability Index, together with your own awareness of strengths and weaknesses, will suggest that you review several of the initiatives. In addition, you will likely want to refer to some of them, when you get a nagging feeling one of them is being called for. The indicators associated with each initiative will help you determine if and when you need to don your leadership hat.

Acknowledging accomplishment is the last of the ten leadership initiatives. Though it marks the end of what might be termed the leadership cycle, it is just *part* of your ongoing leadership development. There's more to come, and that's the focus of Part Three.

PART THREE

Your Ongoing
Leadership Development

SECTION 1

Putting Leadership Style into Action

Putting all ten leadership initiatives into play, using your own natural style, will certainly make you a more effective and authentic leader. You will be leveraging your leadership style by more effectively performing those initiatives that come naturally to you. You will also benefit from your awareness of those initiatives you weren't doing well, or weren't doing at all before. Improving on what you already do, and adding some new leadership initiatives to your daily routine will create a quantum leap in your leadership ability. However, mastering the information in this book is just the *beginning* of your leadership development.

There are at least four additional ways to leverage your leadership style and use the knowledge, skills, and information from the previous chapters to continue your leadership development. You can:

- Leverage your natural ability—managing your strengths and weaknesses.
- Leverage the natural ability of others—letting their interpersonal strengths complement your own.

- Practice "behavioral bridging"—using your awareness of leadership styles to more easily establish rapport with others.

- Use the ten leadership initiatives as a framework for personal development.

Leveraging Your Natural Abilities

The leadership game is more like stud poker than draw poker because you have to play the cards as they are dealt and cannot discard and draw others. The hand you're dealt is usually mixed—good cards and bad. So far in our discussion, the focus has been on leveraging your innate leadership ability, your strengths. But along with that comes the realization that you also have weaker areas. And, as in stud poker, you can't "discard" those weaknesses. Knowing which initiatives don't come naturally, and learning to develop them, gives you an advantage over others seeking to improve their leadership abilities.

You're likely avoiding those initiatives that don't come naturally to you. So, knowing which initiatives are troublesome (or invisible) allows you to put them into play intentionally. It will take time, to be sure, and it will be frustrating as you substitute newly acquired initiatives for previously ineffective or trouble-some behavior. As you do, you will find yourself going through three stages of development and awareness: awareness *after* you act, awareness *as* you act, and finally awareness *before* you act.

The first stage of development is especially frustrating be-cause, initially, your awareness of weaker initiatives will surface *after* you have failed to act. You'll initially respond to many situations the way you always have—and later, wish you had responded differently. Don't be too hard on yourself because you'll soon find yourself in the second stage of development—catching

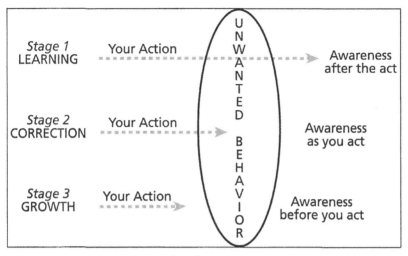

Stage 1 LEARNING	Your Action	U N W A N T E D B E H A V I O R	Awareness after the act
Stage 2 CORRECTION	Your Action		Awareness as you act
Stage 3 GROWTH	Your Action		Awareness before you act

Behavioral Awareness

yourself in the midst of your old behavior and shifting gears. You'll catch yourself doing the same old thing, then you'll stop and intentionally put one of the ten initiatives into play. For example, if you have a coaching leadership style and someone on your team suggests reorganizing and restructuring the operation, you will likely, at first, reject their suggestion. However, knowing that the renewing initiative is a weaker one for your leadership style may enable you to catch yourself rejecting their restructuring proposal out-of-hand. You can then stop your "automatic behavior" and give the suggestion to reorganize and restructure proper consideration. You may still reject it. However, that rejection would be a reasoned and rational decision, and not an impulsive one driven by your dislike for change and for creating problems for people.

As the graphic above indicates in Stage 3, your awareness of your weaker initiatives will come into your awareness *before* you act. This signals a genuine behavioral change on your part. One that is here to stay.

Kim Krisco

As you leverage your awareness of those initiatives that are weaker for you, and practice them, you will eventually become more proficient and more competent. In the end, you will be turning a weakness into a strength. You will be able to play all the cards you've been dealt, even those that may be causing problems for you today.

Leveraging the Natural Ability of Others

Another way to leverage your knowledge of leadership style is to make use of the natural ability of colleagues and team members. This shouldn't be hard to do, since most teams represent some mix of the leadership styles. If you're not naturally adept at one or more of the leadership initiatives, find people on your team who are, and enlist their help. Continuing with the earlier example, if your coaching style makes renewing difficult, ask a Commander-style teammate to lead the reorganization effort or coach and advise you, as you do it. Ideally you want to find a colleague who has a Natural Ability ranking of eight or higher in those initiatives where your ranking is three or lower. The Natural Ability Index chart at the beginning of Part Two can help you identify those leadership styles that you can leverage to offset your weaker areas. Once you have that knowledge, your next task is to identify the leadership styles of your colleagues. A review of the leadership profiles in Part One can help, but there are also some shortcuts that can help you quickly determine someone's leadership styles.

Professional poker players use something they call a "tell" to give them an advantage and to help them win. A tell is an unconscious behavior pattern that tips an opponent off to what's going on with another player. For instance, some players might light up a cigarette when they are bluffing. Others might drum their fingers on the table when holding a big hand. There are also tells with regard to leadership style. By observing or recalling the behavior of your colleagues, you can determine their leadership styles. There are some basic behavioral signs—overall tendencies—that can tip you off to someone's leadership style:

- In general, Strategists and Commanders are more task-oriented, while Coaches and Performers are more people-oriented.

- Performers and Commanders tend to be more extroverted, while Coaches and Strategists are more introverted.

- Commanders and Performers tend to take over when they're with a group of people, while Strategists and Coaches tend to sit back quietly.

- Coaches and Performers prefer to work with others, while Strategists and Commanders prefer to work alone.

There's always the possibility that one particular style dominates on your team. Indeed, it's quite likely because a team has a natural tendency to "homogenize." Since people with similar styles work together more comfortably as the team evolves, it attracts and retains individuals with the same style. This is normal and natural, but not necessarily healthy.

The tendency to like those who have a style similar to our own has some advantages, because individuals with similar styles operate the same way: they make decisions the same way, have fewer conflicts, and create less stress. However this "sameness" has disadvantages as well.

A team composed primarily of people with similar styles magnifies the weaknesses of that particular style. For example, if yours were a team of Performers, you would have difficulty getting anything done. The natural enthusiasm of your teammates, while beneficial on the front end of an undertaking, would eventually wane; detailed action planning would be slow in coming. In this situation, your team would be hard-pressed to achieve quick results. Performers usually cope with this tendency not to follow through by delegating managerial tasks. However a team of Performers would have no one to delegate to. Keep in mind that Performers aren't being singled out here. All the leadership styles have their own particular weaknesses.

To combat this situation of having a one-style team, you should welcome style diversity to teams you lead, and leverage that diversity to give you a competitive advantage. Of course, leading a diverse team of individuals brings with it another set of challenges. Leadership style differences among team members can work to the benefit of your organization, only if the team members learn to respect and to work with one another. This fact brings us to yet another way to leverage your awareness and knowledge of leadership style—behavioral bridging.

Behavioral Bridging: Establishing Rapport with Others

Behavioral bridging involves suspending your own natural leadership style, assessing the style of the individual(s) you're interacting with, and then intentionally shifting into *their* styles long enough to establish rapport. Behavioral bridging is based upon the awareness that we all like working with people who are like ourselves—people who share our style. You intuitively use this awareness whenever you try to make a good impression on someone. With behavioral bridging you are doing the same thing, but doing it more consciously, and with much more information about how to act.

The knowledge you have gained about leadership style allows you to more precisely select those behaviors that will appeal to another person. For example, while you would not have attached the "Commander" label to your boss before reading this book, you would undoubtedly have known that he or she was action-oriented and liked to get down to business. In preparing to meet with such a person, you might:

- Expect a short meeting, probably less than 20 minutes;
- Expect little or no socializing at the meeting;
- Expect to leave the meeting with an assignment and work.

Once you get familiar with the various leadership styles, you'll be able to do far more than just know what to expect. You'll be able to adopt a new set of behaviors that will appeal to a Commander, or a colleague with any other leadership style.

At first, behavioral bridging might appear to be manipulative, but it really isn't. It's not an effective way to fool another person. It takes a lot of energy and concentration to be someone you're not. If you try to use behavioral bridging as a facade, you'll eventually slip up and damage the relationship because you'll show up as a phony.

The intention behind behavioral bridging is not to deceive, but to establish quick rapport—to create a solid interpersonal bond with another person. Once rapport has been established, you can shift back into your own natural style. When you do so, you will find that the other people automatically reciprocate. They begin interacting with you in your preferred leadership style. In this way, behavioral bridging becomes a kind of "personality dance," with you leading.

Behavioral bridging not only contributes to your leadership development by enabling you to build a stronger leadership team to support you, but it gives you an additional tool to use when practicing the modeling and bridging initiatives. Both of those initiatives require that you quickly connect with others and open a clear channel of communication with them. Behavioral bridging allows you to make that proverbial "good first impression."

The following lists offer some tips to help you with behavioral bridging. They will be useful in planning your interactions with people of differing leadership styles.

♦ **When interacting with a Commander . . .**

- Plan on a relatively short meeting.
- Get to the point with little or no small talk.
- Expect to keep the pace of the meeting fast.
- Focus on getting results quickly.
- Avoid using emotional appeals.
- Understand that to get the Commander's support, you will need to continue to keep him or her included and/or advised. If possible, provide a list of possible actions and let the Commander decide how best to proceed.
- Close the meeting with a promise of quick action and personal accountability.

♣ **When interacting with a Strategist . . .**

- Expect the meeting to be slightly longer than usual.
- Kick off the meeting with a well-organized written or oral agenda. If possible, send the agenda out ahead of the meeting.
- Keep the meeting moving at a moderate pace and allow time for questions.
- Focus on the quality and reliability of your approach or process.

- Stick with the agenda. Don't include other business or issues.
- To get the Strategist's support, present all the nitty-gritty details. Include as much written documentation (for instance, charts, graphs) as you can.
- Close the meeting with assurances that your effort is well-planned and organized, and that nothing will go wrong.

♥ **When interacting with a Coach . . .**

- Plan on a meeting of average length or one slightly longer than average.
- Ease into the meeting. Acknowledge and express appreciation for something the Coach has recently done for you or for someone else.
- Gradually accelerate the pace as the meeting moves forward.
- Focus on the need for cooperation.
- Avoid pushy, threatening, or controlling behavior.
- To get the Coach's support, make clear how your project will benefit people. Express your commitment to collaboration and teamwork.
- Close the meeting by requesting the Coach's help. Make sure the Coach knows you value his or her friendship and loyalty.

♠ **When interacting with a Performer . . .**

- Plan on a long meeting. If possible, meet for lunch prior to the meeting or make it a meeting over lunch.

- At the start of the meeting, begin with plenty of small talk. Ask questions. Let the Performer do most of the talking.

- Keep the meeting fast-moving, friendly, and fun.

- Focus on the Performer's role and its importance.

- Avoid a highly detailed presentation. Don't take other calls or hold side discussions with others during the interaction.

- To get the Performer's support, emphasize how the effort will get attention and notoriety.

- Close the meeting by showing that other notable and/ or important individuals support the effort under discussion.

Using your knowledge of leadership style to enhance your relationships with superiors, colleagues, direct reports, and other stakeholders is one of the most powerful ways to leverage the information from previous chapters. However, there is one final way to leverage the ten leadership initiatives and use them to aid your ongoing personal development.

Using the Leadership Initiatives as a Guide for Personal Development

There is a thin line, if one exists at all, between leadership development and personal development. As you recall, the ten initiatives form a leadership process—a "sustainability cycle." Implementing the ten initiatives over and over again results in the long-term growth and the sustained success of your enterprise. Personal development is a growth process not unlike organizational development. Your personal life is a series of growth cycles also. It shouldn't be surprising, then, that the model for leadership development—the ten leadership initiatives—can also serve as a model for your personal development.

Each one of the initiatives has a personal application. You can use the basic concept behind each of the ten initiatives to learn more about yourself. By doing so, you will become aware not only of strengths and weaknesses, but also of critical elements that may be missing. Let's start with the first one.

Personal Development Initiative 1

Personal Envisioning applies to individuals just as envisioning does to organizations. Indeed, your wholehearted commitment to your organization's vision is only possible if it parallels your personal vision. Without this connection, an organizational vision becomes mere words. You can create this link by personal envisioning. To get in touch with your personal vision, remember it should have the same attributes as an organizational vision. Your personal vision should:

- Be specific in time
- Be measurable in some tangible way
- Be challenging and exciting

Write your personal vision down in one or two sentences. Be sure the wording is clear, compelling, and easy to remember. Place it someplace you will look every day—a bathroom mirror, the inside cover of your calendar, etc. This personal vision will give you direction and keep you from being tossed around on the waves of day-to-day circumstances. A ship without a destination is just adrift. Your personal vision will serve as a rudder to keep you on course.

Personal Development Initiative 2

Managing Personal Mindsets refers to your frame of reference, or how you see the world. Your frame of reference influences your behavior. It especially affects how you treat others. Simply defining your frame of reference will put you in touch with the source of many troublesome personal behaviors. Identifying your overall feelings about the world, and the people in it, will make you aware of attitudes and beliefs you may want to examine and change. For example, it is not uncommon for people I coach to hold a general belief that people are basically lazy and one has to use a "carrot and stick" approach to get things done. The idea is that you must dangle a carrot—a reward—on a stick in front of them in order to get what you want. And, if that doesn't work, you hit them with the stick. If you hold this belief, you're going to treat people as if they were jackasses. And while the carrot and stick approach might get the job done for a while, it does severe damage to personal relationships. If you adhere to the carrot and stick philosophy, you may want to examine and change your frame of reference.

To manage personal mindsets, simply ask yourself these questions:

- Do you see people as basically lazy or as industrious?
- Are most people you know good or bad?
- Are most individuals you meet self-serving or other-directed?
- Is the world a treacherous, friendly, or indifferent place?
- Are you basically lovable, or not so lovable?
- Do you feel you can control your own destiny, or do you believe that you're at the mercy of outside forces?

Think of other questions, or have a conversation about your beliefs and attitudes with a close friend. There are many ways to explore your frame of reference and begin to manage your limiting beliefs and mindsets. This exercise would be important to do before taking the next self-development step—modeling.

Personal Development Initiative 3

Personal Modeling connects you with your stakeholders. On a personal level these would include your family, friends, colleagues, and neighbors. Your company is only one of many groups or communities to which you belong. Your personal fulfillment depends on how successful you are in *all* the areas of your life and how adept you are at integrating and balancing the needs of your many stakeholders.

Unfortunately, it is all too common for leaders, successful by every business standard, to reach the pinnacle of their careers and still feel they have failed because they don't have anyone with whom to share their success. A single-minded focus on business success usually alienates and drives away personal stakeholders— your spouse, your children, and your friends.

Regardless of your age or circumstances, it's always a good idea to pause for a moment to take a mental inventory of the people in your life. Don't just count the number, but reflect on the quality of your relationship with each one. What would your life be without them? What would their lives be without you? How important are these relationships? Do you spend an adequate amount of time with each of them, given their importance to you and yours to them?

As you identify and reflect on your stakeholders, be sure to include yourself among them. It is possible to meet the needs of your organization, as well as those of your personal stakeholders, at the expense of your own needs. If this happens, you come face to face with a sad situation—being very successful and feeling totally unfulfilled. Clarifying your personal values can help you avoid this common trap.

Personal Development Initiative 4

Clarifying Personal Values may be the single most important personal development initiative. Just as values influence organizational behavior, values are also a primary driver of personal behavior. In fact, a thorough inventory of your personal values often leads to developmental breakthroughs in your personal life.

What's the most important thing in your life? If you don't know, it's going to be difficult for you to be happy and fulfilled. It's tough enough to get what you want when you know what you're going after; it's nearly impossible when you don't. Identifying your values gives you direction and helps you know how you need to live your life. It enables you to live *with purpose.*

While there are several values-assessment tools available, a self-developed values list provides a good start in inventorying your values. Two additional steps may prove helpful, once you have this list. First, review your list, separating those values which are *really* yours, from those to which you only give lip service. Once you have the "final" list, *rank* your values. This last step is especially important because you'll undoubtedly have a long list of values. Ranking your values allows you to focus on ways to achieve your top three or four. This awareness and focus alone will begin to change your behavior. Your actions, then, will begin to come into alignment with your top three or four values, putting you well on the path to personal fulfillment.

Personal Development Initiative 5

Personal Aligning is the ability to move decisively toward your vision. Once you have a personal vision, it might seem that the next step is to look for opportunities that allow you to move closer to your vision. It's almost as though you're waiting for a door to open. However, if you take this wait-and-see tack, not much will happen. Waiting for the "right opportunity" will actually keep you from achieving your personal vision.

Opportunities usually present themselves only after you have started taking action. It is your action that *creates* opportunities. It requires a leap of faith. You must take steps toward your vision without knowing if you'll be supported. Making this leap of faith is not easy, because, if you're like most people, you have many little voices in your head cautioning, admonishing, and warning you not to move too quickly but to wait for a *real* opportunity.

The little voices in your head aren't bad; they're just uncertain and frightened of failing. This is the time when personal aligning comes in. As you would with a diverse team of individuals, you must first acknowledge each voice inside you, as though it were a separate person. In a way it is; it is one aspect of your personality. You will discover that simply listening to each of the little voices inside will quiet them, and eventually bring them into alignment with your personal vision. It is only when they are all chattering away at the same time that they create a loud, confusing din. As you come to terms with each of the little critics inside, you will begin to act more decisively—with purpose and conviction. You will then be well on your way to achieving your personal vision.

Personal Development Initiative 6

Personal Bridging is based on the realization that achieving your personal vision will almost certainly depend on your ability to enlist the aid of others. In personal development terms, bridging is the process of identifying the people who can help you achieve your personal vision, and then seeking their help.

A vision suddenly becomes more doable if and when others begin to help, that is, when others believe in your vision. Whatever your vision is, you already know people who can be resources for you. For example, an accountant friend of mine is pursuing a vision of operating a recreation center for inner-city youth. When he shared his vision with me, I put him into a bridging mode by asking, "Who do you know that might be able to help?" At first he was stumped, but then people's names began to bubble up—his old football coach lived nearby, a friend of ours was a social worker, and I knew business leaders who might be willing to make monetary contributions. Once we had a list of people who might help, the process of engaging each one in his vision quest could begin.

The following simple three-step enrollment process, which works within organizations, can also be applied in your personal life. Indeed, my friend had intuitively enrolled me by asking these three questions:

- What do you think of my vision?

  This question got me personally involved in his vision. I was able to see that we shared many of the same values and that I might be able to put my values into action by helping him achieve his vision.

- Who do you think might be able to help me?

  I brainstormed with my friend to generate a list of people he knew who might help. His question to me was a tactful way of inviting me to pitch in. And it worked.

- Exactly what might you do to help me?

  This request motivated me to act. This last step is critical to the bridging process, because the objective of bridging is action, not idle conversation. I offered to call three business and community leaders I knew to ask them if their companies would make donations to a youth recreation center.

While starting an inner-city recreation center seems like an easy sell, I can tell you that my friend encountered many problems along the way. It was at this point that the next personal development initiative was put into play.

Personal Development Initiative 7

Managing Personal Breakdowns is similar to managing breakdowns on an organizational level. Paraphrasing an old aphorism: Problems are life showing up. You should not only *expect* to encounter problems on your way to achieving your vision; you should see them as positive evidence that you are moving closer to your vision. Problems often point out new ways to achieve your vision. Unfortunately, problems are discouraging and may result in your compromising your vision. By managing breakdowns, you can hold firm to your original vision. Circumstances may change the means, but your personal vision remains constant.

Managing personal breakdowns involves identifying and removing the barriers to cooperation. What is keeping someone from assisting you? Identify the barrier, then remove it. Continuing with my earlier example, when I called client-friends to ask for donations to a youth recreation center, none of them came through. However, by applying a managing breakdowns methodology, I was able to see and eliminate barriers that were keeping me from enlisting the aid of business sponsors. Some of these barriers included a lack of tangibility and the fact that I was only asking for dollars. In response, my friend and I produced a videotape and drafted a written proposal. Those efforts made the vision real and tangible. We also asked for *help,* not dollars, and we found that many individuals were willing and able to contribute in many non-monetary ways.

Personal Development Initiative 8

Personal Coaching is the key to accelerating your leadership development. As a leadership initiative, coaching is something you give to others—a way for you to keep people you work with in action and moving toward your vision. Personal coaching is, however, something you seek for yourself—it's coaching you receive.

Engaging a coach may be the best way to continue improving your personal and professional development. The next section is devoted entirely to finding and working with a personal coach. A more in-depth exploration of this kind of coaching can wait until then. For now, it is sufficient to think of a coach as a "mirror," reflecting your assumptions, feelings, and behaviors. The reflection of this mirror is candid feedback. It gives you awareness, and with it the ability to choose new and different paths forward. It is this ability to choose, along with the choices you will make, that will ensure continuous growth and development.

Personal Development Initiative 9

Personal Renewing acknowledges that we all operate within a series of life cycles. Within your own lifetime, you obviously go through the processes of birth, growth, maturity, and death. However, within your lifetime, you will experience shorter cycles of birth, growth, and death. It is because of these natural birth, growth, and death cycles that personal renewing is needed. Your life's work is one example of how growth cycles show up during your lifetime.

On the average, a person has four or five careers in a lifetime. The infamous "Peter Principle" could be thought of as life cycles at work. In any given position or job, a point of maximum competence is reached, followed by decline. Ideally one moves on to another position and/or career. Failing that, the decline in productivity and efficiency continues unabated. Personal renewing, when applied to your career cycles, makes you more aware of your performance and helps you to make a career change consciously, when *you* see a decline in effectiveness. That change might be a totally new career, or just finding a way to breathe new life into your existing job. Renewing can be applied in other aspects of your life as well, and in particular within relationships.

The primary relationships in your life go through growth cycles. A relationship is "born," it then grows, matures, and—unless you renew it—will die. The indicators that a relationship needs renewal are not mysterious. When you choose to spend less and less time with an individual and/or your conversations become mostly a rehash of the same old subjects, renewal is probably needed. The personal renewal process begins with an awareness that leads to a conscious decision to revitalize and recharge. From there you fashion a new vision. In the case of a personal relationship, your shared vision might include building a greenhouse, or teaming up to teach a Sunday school class, or volunteering at the local girls and boys club.

Is it time for personal renewal?

Personal Development Initiative 10

Acknowledging Personal Accomplishment is more than just rewarding yourself; it is accepting the acknowledgment you get from others. You're probably getting more acknowledgment than you think.

When I ask people if they regularly acknowledge others, about 80 percent say that they do. But when I ask if *they* receive acknowledgment, only 20 percent say they do. This seeming paradox exists because most of us don't hear or don't accept personal acknowledgment. To make matters worse, we give away much of the acknowledgment we get. Watch what happens when you compliment others. More than half the time they will say, "I was just lucky," "No big deal," or "Anybody could have done it." These self-deprecating words diminish the power and impact of acknowledgment. Learn to accept thanks and appreciation from others. When you are acknowledged, just say "Thank you." Saying those two words, and adding nothing more, is the first step to acknowledging your own personal accomplishment.

The Path to Leadership Mastery

There is a positive, dynamic tension that exists between personal development and leadership development. As with leadership development, personal development is greatly enhanced by a process in which you systematically explore your strengths and your weaknesses—capitalizing on your strengths and managing your weaknesses. Whether you use the ten initiatives as a framework or not, take time for personal introspection. Once you bridge the gap between personal and leadership development, you will have addressed many of the barriers standing between you and leadership mastery, and will have mastered the following behaviors:

- You will be aware that the true source of your power as a leader comes from within.

- You will be able to continue to use the ten initiatives, and other systems of exploration and awareness, to continue your development.

- You will gain an appreciation for the key elements driving your leadership and personal behavior—vision, mindsets, values, renewal, and acknowledgment. More importantly, you will be able to leverage these elements to improve your effectiveness.

- You will be on your way to mastering a new set of tools and techniques that will allow you to create a more powerful future—modeling, aligning, bridging, managing breakdowns, and coaching.

At this point you're hopefully seeing the real possibility of becoming more and more successful in the leadership game. What you've learned so far will help you win a lot of hands. To ensure that you win the game, and continue winning future games, you need to take part in *continuous* leadership development. The most powerful tool you'll need to continue your leadership development is coaching, because it focuses on the two things from which all change emanates: awareness and choice.

SECTION 2

Personal Coaching:
Key to Ongoing Development

I believe that the greatest single tool for one's ongoing leadership and personal development is personal coaching. As a leadership initiative, coaching is something you offer to others. However, to grow as a leader, you must seek coaching for yourself. Coaching is well recognized in sports and the arts as an important way to improve personal performance. Over the last two decades, coaching has become accepted in business. Specifically, personal coaching:

- Allows you to develop a useful understanding of yourself—the reasons you think the way you do, why you tend to behave the way you do, and what you need to be successful, happy, and fulfilled.

- Enables you to distinguish between who you really are and the image you have created of yourself.

- Reveals your previously unseen options and choices—new directions and opportunities that may lead to greater success and fulfillment.

- Improves self-worth and overall confidence in your ability to perform.

- Enables you to take charge of your life and your future.

While coaching is often focused on business issues, it is not a traditional problem-solving process. It focuses on what is going on *inside* you, rather than what's happening around you. Coaching is an *introspective dialogue*. We are more accustomed to looking *outside* ourselves for answers, knowledge, and guidance. So, looking inward may be somewhat new for some of you.

Being open to personal coaching requires courage. Most of us have no idea what we will find if and when we look inside ourselves. Adding to that fear, our ego generates endless reasons why we don't need or want personal coaching. Working with another person, a coach, someone who is committed to your growth and development, will reduce your fear and accelerate the learning process. In addition to reducing the fear of looking inside, a coach adds an element of accountability. Personal coaching is based on the belief that you are totally responsible for your own development, and ultimately your own success and fulfillment.

A personal coach provides one other important dimension— an outside perspective. One reason you may have trouble dealing with personal issues is that you are too close to yourself. It's like trying to look at your own face. Think about it. You can feel your face with your hands or ask someone to describe your face, but those exercises will yield only vague approximations. Even after much tactile exploration and many descriptions from others, you would only have a vague picture of what you look like. Obviously, you don't have to feel your face to know what you look like. You can look in a mirror. In essence, that's what a coach is, a mirror reflecting emerging awareness and ideas back to you in words, rather than pictures.

Think about looking into a mirror. If you do so for any length of time, you will go through four stages that are similar to the four stages you go through as you are being coached.

Stage 1

Looking in a mirror: Initially, you *focus softly* on your image. You look at the image in the glass, but don't actually see it. It is as though you have an image in your mind as to what you look like, and that image is what you initially see.

Working with a coach: You will initially focus on distinguishing between who you really are versus the elaborate stories you have made up about yourself—stories usually created to explain or justify a problem behavior.

Stage 2

Looking in a mirror: Your mind's image begins to fade away and you see your face as it really is. This can be a disturbing experience, since you will not only see your better features, but your "blemishes" as well. Staring at that reflection, you become aware of what you really look like.

Working with a coach: You begin to come to grips with who you really are. You see your strengths and weaknesses; you become aware of disturbing feelings and tendencies; and you may recognize and acknowledge your special qualities and gifts. Over time, you can make peace with yourself as you really are, and explore ways to change or manage those things you don't feel good about.

Stage 3

Looking in a mirror: As you continue to gaze into the mirror, your focus begins to change. You will see not only yourself, but will begin to notice other images in the mirror—you see the room you are in and others who are in the room.

Working with a coach: You will begin to explore your relationship to circumstances, your environment, and people. New options, opportunities, and choices reveal themselves. This expansion tends to put you into action or, at least, inclined to act.

Stage 4

Looking in a mirror: You decide to put the glass aside and prepare to meet the day.

Working with a coach: You will realize an almost limitless number of options and choices that surfaced during your introspective dialogue; you can choose to approach action in a way that leverages your strengths, minimizes your weaknesses, and makes you show up in new and better ways.

After this experience, you'll likely never look at a mirror in the same way again. While perhaps a bit dramatic, this metaphor should provide you with a gut-level understanding of the coaching process. Coaching begins with awareness and ends with action. You should judge the effectiveness of your personal coach, in part, by the actions you are taking and the results you are achieving. Coaching should show up in tangible and measurable ways.

Choosing and Creating Coaching Relationships

Because coaching has become a recognized and accepted way to improve individual and organizational performance, you now have access to a good number of professional business coaches. If you decide to seek the services of a professional business coach, be sure you are getting a coach and not an advisor, consultant, or therapist. Your coach should be able to communicate his or her approach to coaching in a few simple sentences. Remember: whatever the approach, the coaching process should end with your going into action.

In addition to being coached yourself, you should ask your coach to transfer his or her coaching skills to you. A simple way to do this is to end a coaching session by asking the coach to explain the process used during the previous session. Those committed to coaching are not possessive of their knowledge and will gladly share it. However, seeking an outside professional coach is not the only way to get personal coaching.

When looking for a coach, don't ignore the obvious. You can ask a close friend and confidant to be your coach. As in many sports, coaching techniques are easy to learn, but take practice and time to master. Still, since coaching is a conversation, everyone has the basic means to be a coach. And, because it is simply a structured conversation, coaching and its techniques can also be learned. Even operating at a "beginner level," coaching will produce huge improvements.

If a close friend agrees to coach you, you can use this book as a guide to select the areas you wish to explore. You should:

1. Focus on those areas where you feel you are weakest. The Natural Ability Index will be a helpful guide. Concentrate on those leadership initiatives for which you were rated three or less.

2. Ask your new coach to read the short sections in this book about each of the initiatives that you wish to improve. Your coach should prepare a list of open-ended questions to ask you. The answers to these questions might reveal strengths and weaknesses, as well as new opportunities for you to actually practice the initiative.

3. Tell your coach you want to end each coaching conversation committed to taking a specific action or actions.

Asking a close friend to coach you can be frustrating at first, but it is a great learning experience. The frustration you might both experience comes from misunderstandings you and others may have about coaching. Indeed, it is often confused with advice or instruction. However, coaching deals with an area of knowledge that can be called "fugitive awareness."

If you wish to continue on this developmental path, my recommendation is to find a coach. However, as your self-awareness grows, you will gradually get to a place where a dedicated personal coach may not be necessary.

Your Changing Relationship to Coaching

Until you've been in a coaching relationship for some time, it is difficult to appreciate the impact it can have on your life. It is truly a transformational tool.

As you are coached, you will find that you "automatically" begin doing things differently and, as a consequence, achieve different results. In particular, your relationship with others improves dramatically. This positive reinforcement causes you to seek coaching again and again, or to seek more powerful coaches. The graphic on the next page shows how your relationship to coaching changes over time.

As you continue to grow and evolve, coaching will begin to affect you at deeper levels—changing your mindsets, your values, and even your beliefs. When this shift occurs, the world begins to change because you perceive it differently. You will understand and appreciate what psychologists, philosophers, and poets have been saying since the beginning of time, that we each live in a separate world of our own making. Change your perception, and you change your world. This is not an exaggeration. We have all experienced such powers of perception.

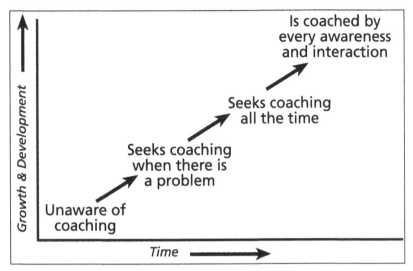

Evolution of coaching

Your perceptions are continually changed through experience. For example, a friend of mine, who had lived in a small, rural Midwestern town most of his life, spent some time with me in the Rocky Mountains. He came to Colorado's high country with a set of expectations, beliefs, and mindsets. He expected everyone to dress and look like someone on the cover of a REI or L.L.Bean catalog. He was hesitant to go for hikes in the mountains for fear of mountain lions, bears, and snakes.

However, after a couple of weeks, I saw a change in his perceptions of Colorado. He discovered that people who choose to live in the mountains are an eclectic and highly diverse group. He bought his first pair of good hiking boots and began taking long hikes and decided he wanted to climb some of the "fourteeners" (the 53 mountains in Colorado exceeding 14,000 feet in elevation). He went home exploring the possibility of relocating to Colorado. What had happened? Experience changed his mindsets beliefs, and even some of his values. In a few weeks' time, Colorado went from a strange place full of potential dangers to a place he would eventually call home. It wasn't Colorado that had changed, it was his *perception* of it.

Coaching has the same power to change your perceptions, with less stress and in much less time than it took my friend to don his hiking boots. What's more, coaching allows you to access limiting mindsets and beliefs that would be difficult or impossible to change through direct experience. In this way, being coached accelerates both your personal and your leadership growth and development.

The exploration of personal coaching nearly brings to a close our coaching relationship. It seems appropriate that we end this phase of your leadership development the way I end many of my coaching relationships—with a few select coaching tips discussed in the next section.

SECTION 3

One Final Hand

When I'm playing poker with my friends, the last hand dealt is called showdown. Each player receives five cards, faceup. Whoever is dealt the best hand wins. In one sense, this chapter is our last hand. So let me deal one last card to you. On that card you'll find some parting advice—three tips that will make the biggest difference in your ongoing leadership development.

With these parting tips *our* coaching relationship comes to an end, but this is not the end of your leadership development. I have tried to heighten your awareness of what leaders do, when and how they do it. Most importantly, you are now aware of your innate leadership style, an awareness that enables you to leverage your strengths and manage your weaknesses. I will leave you with the one thought I leave with all my clients: *awareness* is the key to personal effectiveness and ongoing growth.

As you lead, be aware of what is happening, why, and how it is happening. Then act accordingly. Most of all, recognize what is happening *inside* yourself. This knowledge will be your best guide. The true source of your leadership ability lies within you. Trust your gut. Build upon your awareness. Seek opportunities that will put your leadership ability to the test. Here are a few parting tips:

Coaching Tips for the COMMANDER

- Focus on influence, not control. Your need to be in control is probably the biggest contributor to strained personal and professional relationships. Do more asking and less telling. Be patient. You have good instincts and your decisions are right much of the time. Give other people more time to see things your way.

- Give time and energy to others in your life. While you seem to thrive on hard work and long hours, your demanding schedule leaves little room for others—particularly those closest to you. Professional success is important, but make sure there are people in your life to celebrate and share your accomplishments.

- Stop playing the strong silent type. The ability to be vulnerable at times is a trait that distinguishes great leaders. Sharing your feelings and asking for help when you're down are hard to do; but such openness works wonders for relationships. It will bring you closer to others and get you acting sooner.

Coaching Tips for the STRATEGIST

- Work with others more. Almost any group of people would benefit from your objective observations and ideas. If you don't feel welcome or comfortable offering your ideas, it may have more to do with the way you contribute your ideas and suggestions rather than what you are actually saying.

- Balance your feedback—be less critical. Your ability to see what's missing is a gift, but people need to hear what's working, too. When you have concerns and reactions, don't make them personal. Present feedback as one member of the team—not as someone standing on the outside looking in.

- Take action sooner. You'll never be 100% sure, and you'll probably never stop worrying, so take action when you're 90% sure. Contrary to how you might feel, decisions are seldom totally wrong or totally right. You can usually make small adjustments and corrections, if you miss the mark slightly. Remember, there's a cost to inaction.

Coaching Tips for the COACH

- Walk the line between caring and care-taking. While people may have come to expect more from you when they ask for help, committed listening and gentle coaching with little or no personal involvement are the best responses. Beyond that, you risk sacrificing your needs for someone else's. If you do, you'll often resent others and feel bad about yourself.

- Put any criticism you receive in perspective. Criticism and feedback are someone's assessment—not the objective truth. Your unique insights and ideas are needed; don't hold back for fear of criticism or conflict.

- Find ways to manage conflict constructively. Your aversion to conflict doesn't make it go away. If it's not dealt with, conflict will just show up a little later and probably more intensely—and/or it will eat you up inside. There are techniques and processes to deal with conflict. As you learn to practice them, your relationship to conflict will become healthier.

Coaching Tips for the PERFORMER

- Follow through. Few things compare with the excitement of creating and launching a new endeavor, but your efforts are wasted if you don't see the project through. The people you're leading can easily get the message that you don't care, if you don't follow through with the same energy and enthusiasm.

- Don't overcommit yourself. You're so good at starting things, it's easy to find yourself running short on time and energy. Leaders should focus organizational energy and resources—not fragment and disperse them.

- Listen a little more—talk a little less. Guard your tendency to take over during meetings and discussions. When others are speaking, don't use that time to plan what you're going to say next.

ABOUT THE AUTHOR

KIM KRISCO is a semi-retired coach, consultant, and change management specialist. He spent most of his career coaching and facilitating high-performance teams and business executives. He pioneered the field of leadership development based on natural style. His trademark is working with internal teams, who *learn within work*, and designing sabbatical programs for companies.

He founded Transition Technologies in 1990 after leaving a Fortune 100 company where he served as operations trouble-shooter, tackling assignments in problem operations and functions. He led the design and development of a strategic process to support two national reorganizations, the largest merger in telecommunications history, a 30 percent downsizing, and the process reengineering of the entire company.

Kim has a diverse background in corporate communications, public relations, and electronic media production. He has authored several nonfiction books on leadership and coaching, and more recently continues in the footsteps of the master storyteller, Sir Arthur Conan Doyle, by adding several new Sherlock Holmes novels to the canon.

He and his partner, Sara Rose, live in south-central Colorado in a home that they built themselves on the North Fork of the Purgatory River.

You can find out more about Kim and his current activities at www.kimkrisco.com.

At this point in the book, you've hopefully come face to face with what you didn't know about leadership. If I have done my job, then you know that:

- You already have everything you need to be a leader.

- Leadership does not require that you behave a certain way.

- Ten initiatives distinguish leadership from management. If you practice them when they are called for, you will become a powerful leader.

- You have tendencies or preferred ways of thinking and acting, which are barriers to your leadership development and organizational efficiency. By being aware of these tendencies, you can manage them and/or compensate for them by using the natural ability of others in your organization.

- You can leverage your new awareness and knowledge of leadership style to improve your relationship with others.

The time has come to change dealers. Now you have all the cards. It's up to you to seek, to find, and to conquer greater and greater challenges.

I am handing the deck to you. It's your deal.